DECORATING
WITH
DRIED
FLOWERS

DECORATING WITH DRIED FLOWERS

A step-by-step guide

to cultivating, drying, and arranging

dried flowers and plants

MALCOLM HILLIER

Photographs by Andreas Einsiedel

CROWN PUBLISHERS, INC. • NEW YORK

For Peter Day

Art Editor Sally Smallwood
Project Editor Jane Laing
Editorial Consultant Susanna Longley
Designer Tim Foster
American Editor Marjorie J. Dietz

Editorial Director Jackie Douglas
Art Director Roger Bristow

Published in the United States of America
by Crown Publishers, Inc., 225 Park Avenue South,
New York, New York 10003
and represented in Canada by
the Canadian MANDA Group

Originally published in Great Britain
by Dorling Kindersley Limited, London

CROWN is a trademark of Crown Publishers, Inc.

Manufactured in Italy

Library of Congress Cataloguing-in-Publication Data
Hillier, Malcolm.
   Decorating with dried flowers.
   Includes index.
   1. Dried flower arrangement. I. Title.
   SB449.3.D7H545 1988   745.92   87-27411
ISBN 0-517-56923-X

First American Edition

Contents

Introduction

I have been obsessed with plants and flowers since early childhood. It never ceases to amaze me that seeds, varying only a little in size, should produce such an extraordinary variety of different flowers; that one plant can have leaves that are only a sixth of an inch long, while another has great leaves six or more feet long. How can it be? I shall choose never to know, to let it always be simple and wondrous magic.

To work with flowers is one of the most fortunate experiences possible. Each season brings its new excitements. Even on the grayest of winter days, my ceiling glows with hanging bunches of dried flowers. Outside, the first Christmas rose and some winter jasmine hint at what is to come. Spring gathers pace with its scudding clear yellows and showery blues and then suddenly a warm stillness settles and the first peonies and roses are scenting the early summer garden. It is again time to start preparing a glorious succession of flowers for drying.

The pleasure of dried flowers
An enormous amount of plant material can be preserved so that it retains much of its fresh, glowing color and form. It is wonderful to be able to capture summer, perhaps in the shape of a full-petalled peony, or with a perfect rose, knowing that it will still be perfect all through the winter – a testament to those lazy days of sunshine. Roses and peonies are only the first of the summer flowers and leaves that can be preserved. There are the tall spires of cream and pink astilbe followed by even taller delphiniums in all the colors of the sky; there are cornflowers and love-in-a-mist; there are more roses: sweet-scented yellow ones and deep-scented red ones.

The fragrance of dried flowers
I love the summer scents. For scent, more than all the other senses, triggers the happiest of memories for me. Lavender and yarrow, great spicy lilies, silvery aromatic artemisia foliage, ferns growing between the stones, their green smell lying close to the ground, and roses will all continue to fill the room with their perfumes when dry. All evoke beautiful memories of high summer – the garden path leading between flowery borders towards a stream and water meadows beyond. With autumn, the ceilings are full of drying flowers again, deep with all the colors of the rainbow: turning leaves, wood smoke, hydrangeas, Chinese lanterns, seedheads, and the last roses.

The drying process
I prefer to air dry plant material by hanging the stems in bunches on the walls and from the ceiling. In this way they provide decoration as they dry, and are often too beautiful to move. Of course, there are other ways of preserving plant material. Some people enjoy the delicate task of drawing out the moisture from flowers with desiccants like sand and silica gel, alum and borax. Others like to press flowers in a press or book. Foliage like beech and eucalyptus can be preserved with glycerine and many flowers and leaves can be crystallized with sugar and gum arabic or egg white and used to decorate cakes and biscuits.

Arranging dried flowers
All this is only the beginning. Because now comes the wonderful job of combining all the dried ingredients. Deciding on where arrangements are going to look best, choosing containers, getting together interesting collections of dried material in exciting combinations of colors, shapes and textures: arranging is so therapeutic. Time, any worries or troubles, the pressures that surround you are gone and you are aware only of the simple joy of working with flowers. And for me that is always going to be wondrous magic.

Ferny arrangement
*Pressed royal and female ferns,
hosta and mahonia leaves,
desiccant-dried Christmas roses
and air-dried cone twigs are
brought to life with the addition of
some miniature red roses in this
beautiful Chinese copper bowl.*

THE PRINCIPLES OF ARRANGING

A spring-like posy of Helichrysum bracteatum *and* Acacia decurrens dealbata.

A great many elements combine to make an arrangement of flowers, be they dried or fresh, and the most important part of flower arranging is the creative part of it. We all have our own preferences concerning shape, color, texture and pattern, in the same way as we have different tastes in food, and there are no hard and fast rules about how to arrange dried flowers. There are, however, a few guidelines to bear in mind when creating an arrangement.

Arrangements fall into several categories. There are the simplest arrangements of all – bunches of flowers gathered together to make a bouquet or posy. Then there are the more elaborate arrangements without containers, such as wreaths, ropes of flowers, garlands or even brides' or bridesmaids' headdresses. These arrangements are all built on a framework, from a single wire for a headdress, to a moss-filled chicken-wire tube for a wreath. Finally, there are the arrangements created in containers: baskets, bowls, urns, dishes, boxes, jugs, vases in myriad shapes, colors, textures and sizes, can all be used to hold dried plant material.

What then of shape? Shape should be strong and well defined. Curves should be generous and lines obvious, even if they are partly masked by the informal nature of the plant material. The overall shape of the arrangement should not appear cramped, either in itself or when placed in position. Color guidelines are more difficult to give. Any flowers *can* look beautiful in any combination, although you are less likely to create an arrangement that does not work colorwise if you combine flowers of colors that are near to each other in the spectrum. As far as texture is concerned, it is more interesting to offset different textures against one another.

Ingredients

At least eighty per cent of all plants – flowers, foliage and seed-heads – can be preserved to give an enormous variety of plant material that can be used in dried-flower arrangements. Air drying, pressing, chemical drying and preserving with glycerine all extend the "life" of flowers, leaves and seed-heads for at least a year. Of course, some dry more successfully than others: chrysanthemums, carnations and most bulbous plants do not dry well at all.

Ideal plants for drying and arranging
The rose – one of the most common, and special, plants grown throughout the world – takes pride of place for flower arrangers. Fortunately, it dries very well. The hybrid tea rose is easy to air dry (see p. 94) keeping its color very well, while single or open double roses can be dried chemically (see p.100) with silica gel, borax or sand. Delphiniums, including larkspur, most species of yarrow, hydrangeas in their many colors, although the blue and white hydrangea heads are more difficult to dry than the pink and red, are all extremely attractive when dried. *Alchemilla mollis*, baby's breath, all the well known helichrysum, onion flowers and seed-heads, and statice also all look beautiful when dried and are therefore of invaluable use to the dried-flower arranger.

Scented flowers for drying
Then there are the sweet-smelling flowers such as lavender. Lavender absolutely must be cut and hung to dry four or so days before the flowers come out; if it is picked later, the flowers will certainly drop while it is drying. It will continue to emit a beautiful scent for many months after being dried. Mimosa, too, retains its scent once it is dried. Peonies and roses also retain their fragrance, although their perfumes are more elusive. The pretty, delicate, rust-colored flowers and leaves of marjoram dry well: try adding some stems of the herb to an arrangement to give it a special, lingering, aromatic perfume.

Foliage and seed-heads for drying
Most arrangements require foliage to act as a foil for the flowers. Bells of Ireland, the many varieties of eucalyptus, copper beech leaves and ivy can all be preserved using glycerine (see p.102) and you can air dry eucalyptus if you hang it up. You can press most foliage (see p.98), and ferns, beech, oak, maple and poplar are ideal subjects. You can pick them in high summer when the mature stems are in their green state, or in autumn, just as the leaves reach their peak of red, rust, gold or yellow.

Seed-heads add interesting textures to an arrangement. Many seed-heads will dry on the plant without any help from you, but if you want good specimens it is important to pick them just as they reach perfection, before the weather has a chance to spoil them. Poppies, love-in-a-mist, corn-on-the-cob, the seed-heads of grasses and cereals and fir cones are all simple to dry: simply store them in a cool, dry place. Bulrushes and pampas grass both need to be picked well before the seeds mature and start to drop, when they should be fixed by spraying with hair lacquer. You might like to paint them a bright color to make a striking feature in an arrangement. Poppy seed-heads look wonderful sprayed bright red and fir cones are eye-catching sprayed a sparkling silver (see p.107).

Yellow rose
Rosa 'Golden Times'

Pink rose
Rosa 'Silva'

Red rose
Rosa 'Christian Dior'

Royal fern
Osmunda regalis

Silver cypress
Kochia sp.

Large-leaved hydrangea
Hydrangea macrophylla

Eucalyptus
Eucalyptus pauciflora nana

Miniature bulrush
Typha angustifolia

Common beech
Fagus sylvatica

Bells of Ireland or shell flower
Moluccella laevis

Corn-on-the-cob
Zea mays

Old man's beard or traveller's joy
Clematis vitalba

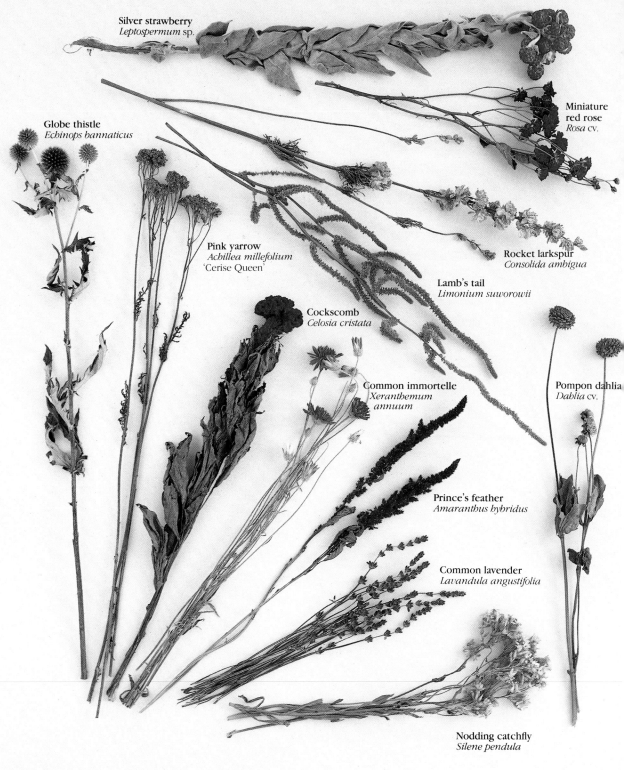

Silver strawberry
Leptospermum sp.

Miniature
red rose
Rosa cv.

Globe thistle
Echinops bannaticus

Pink yarrow
Achillea millefolium
'Cerise Queen'

Rocket larkspur
Consolida ambigua

Lamb's tail
Limonium suworowii

Cockscomb
Celosia cristata

Common immortelle
*Xeranthemum
annuum*

Pompon dahlia
Dahlia cv.

Prince's feather
Amaranthus hybridus

Common lavender
Lavandula angustifolia

Nodding catchfly
Silene pendula

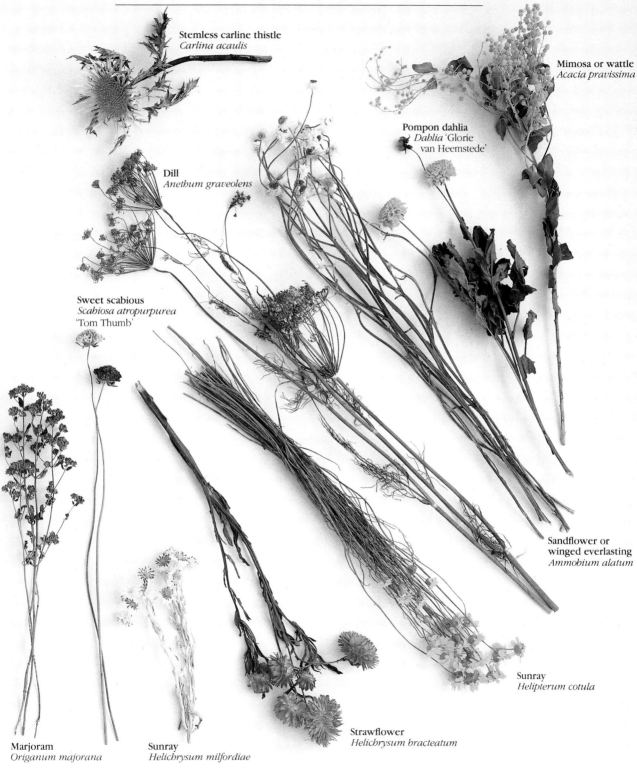

Stemless carline thistle
Carlina acaulis

Mimosa or wattle
Acacia pravissima

Dill
Anethum graveolens

Pompon dahlia
Dahlia 'Glorie van Heemstede'

Sweet scabious
Scabiosa atropurpurea
'Tom Thumb'

Sandflower or
winged everlasting
Ammobium alatum

Sunray
Helipterum cotula

Marjoram
Origanum majorana

Sunray
Helichrysum milfordiae

Strawflower
Helichrysum bracteatum

Wiring Ingredients

Before making an arrangement of dried flowers or foliage it is frequently necessary to wire the flower-heads, leaves or seed-heads. You may need to strengthen fragile stalks, extend stems, or create stems, perhaps for cones. You may also need to wire bunches of plant material. Florist wire is ideal for all these purposes, although you may need to use cane for a particularly heavy-headed flower. Simply select florist wire to suit the thickness and strength of the stem you need to wire and insert it into a hollow stem or bind it to a solid stem, or stems with thin rose wire. Finally, cover both florist and rose wire with floral tape.

Wiring flower-heads
You will need a pair of florists' scissors, the required length of medium-gauge florist wire and a spool of fine rose wire (place it in a cup to keep it from unravelling).

1 *Cut the fragile stem about 3.5cm (1½in) down from the flower-head and discard it. Hold the florist wire against the cut stem so that it touches the underside of the flower-head. Pull some rose wire from the spool.*

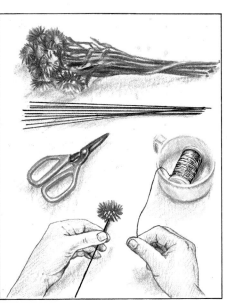

2 *Hold the end of the rose wire at the bottom of the cut stem. Loop it around the stem and florist wire, bending it under the flower-head.*

3 *Wind the rose wire tightly around the stem, florist and rose wire. Cut and wind end in 7.5cm (3in) below the flower.*

To wire a heavy-headed flower, substitute a piece of cane for the florist wire and medium-gauge florist wire for the rose wire.

Lengthening hollow stems

Insert florist wire 5–7.5cm (2–3in) up the inside of the stem to fit snugly.

Wiring cones
You will need heavy-gauge florist wire cut into appropriate stem lengths and a pair of pliers.

1 Push the florist wire through the bottom scales until 5cm (2in) juts out.

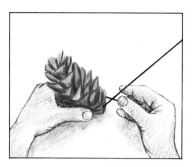

2 Bend the ends of the wire around the cone.

3 Twist the ends of the wire together to secure and bend under the cone. Trim the shorter end with pliers. The long wire forms the stem and should start from the center of the underside of the cone.

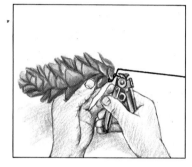

Wiring bunches

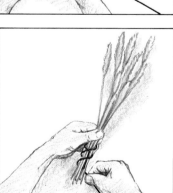

1 Hold a medium-gauge length of florist wire next to the stems, aligning the ends. With the other hand take the wire 5cm (2in) up the stems and bend it behind them.

2 Wind the long end of florist wire down over the short end and the bunch of stems until you reach the bottom of the stems. The rest of the wire forms an extension to the flower stems, so cut when you have sufficient length.

Concealing wire

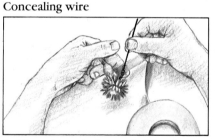

1 Place the end of a spool of floral tape behind the top of the wired stem at an angle of 45°.

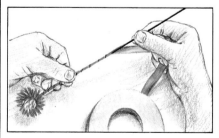

2 Twist the wire so that the tape spirals up it, making sure that the tape overlaps itself so that no wire is showing.

Simple Arrangements

Not only are bouquets and posies the simplest arrangements of dried flowers to make but they also make beautiful presents. Bouquets have a flat back and consist of a fan-shaped bunch of flowers, leaves and seed-heads. These are firmly tied together with wire, which is then covered with ribbon or raffia, leaving a group of stalks below the tie. Posies have a circular head of flowers and can be arranged formally, as the Victorians were fond of doing, or in a wilder manner.

Bouquets

Choosing dried plant material for a bouquet is a very simple matter: most flowers look attractive in combination. Keeping a sense of proportion in your arrangement is crucial. In a small bouquet, such as the one below, the flowers must not be too large and, if you are including foliage in your arrangement, it too should be small scale. Moreover, its shape, texture and color should act as a foil for the flowers, emphasizing their delicate beauty.

All the colors of the rainbow are available to choose from in dried flowers and the plant material can be used in an infinite number of combinations. Mixed bunches always have an attractive natural quality and you can buy bunches of dried flowers to use in many different mixed bouquets. You may be limited to plants that you have grown and dried yourself but even so, you will probably find that you can create a wide range of flower combinations.

When making a bouquet, always start with the longest piece of plant material and place it in the center. Fan out the flowers from this to produce a curve, overlapping the stems where the tie will be made. Bare stems showing above the tie should be avoided, so make sure that the flowers or leaves descend to the tying position. Use either ribbon, colored string or raffia for the tie and ensure that you tie the stems together firmly so that none can fall out and all the flowers are held in position. Finally, trim the stems to a "V" shape.

Posies

Posies are a little more difficult to make and consist of pieces of dried material bound in one by one, preferably with spool wire, to make an all-round arrangement with a curved top. Again, scale is important and offsetting rounded flowers with spiky material makes an attractive, eye-catching posy.

Once all the flowers are wired together it is usually a good idea to add a ribbon or raffia tie and bow to suit the arrangement. This can be used either to cover the wire or to replace it: any unsightly wire can be carefully cut away once the final tie or bow is in position.

A small, exquisite bouquet makes a lovely present.

Informal posy
Rosa *'Golden Times'*, spires of
mimosa, lemon Helichrysum
bracteatum *and* H. angustifolium,
*a cream scabious and budding
golden rod burst from this
informal posy (left). A filigree of
Spanish moss encircles them
poetically.*

Simple bouquet
*Deep red roses are beautifully set
off by the 'Bristol Fairy' gypsophila
(below).*

Formal posy
*Into a base of greeny-blue
hydrangea flower-heads are
arranged marjoram, small
echinops, cottage scabious and
blue statice (left).*

Arrangements in Containers

When considering creating a flower arrangement most people immediately think of arranging flowers in a container rather than making a garland, a wreath or a dried-flower tree. Perhaps container arrangements are the most popular because they require less preparation than arrangements with bases; perhaps it is because of the diversity of container arrangements that can be created; or perhaps we are simply anxious to display a particularly attractive container. Whatever the reason, it cannot be disputed that beautiful and exceptional arrangements can be created in containers as long as the proportions, shape, color and texture of both the plant material and the container are carefully considered.

Planning arrangements

When creating a container arrangement it is most important that the plant material and container should combine to create a single new identity. A successful arrangement is one in which plant material combines so well with the container that it is impossible to imagine the flowers, seed-heads and foliage without the container and vice versa.

Of course, not only should arrangement and container look stunningly natural together but they should also look wonderful in the location you have chosen for them. In fact, plant material, container and location should be considered equally when planning a container arrangement. Usually, it is best to decide on the position for the arrangement first. Then, bearing in mind the colors and patterns of the wall, carpet, curtains and furnishing fabrics, to choose the container.

Choosing containers

Dried flowers tend to look their best in containers that have a natural quality about them. The colors of dried flowers tend to be slightly muted compared with fresh flowers and consequently look extremely attractive in baskets, earthenware, terracotta, wood and stone containers. If you particularly want to use a china or porcelain vase then pick a more primitive piece without a high-gloss surface and with a soft, rather than hard-edged pattern.

If you dry your own plant material, then the varieties that you have grown or purchased as fresh bunches for drying will affect your choice of container. However, as more and more flower shops are stocking interesting dried material, you can add to your own home-grown selection or even buy everything ready dried. So, if you wish, you can collect only the plant material that features the colors and shapes that work well with your decorative schemes and your range of containers.

A low, ceramic bowl with streaks of colors becomes a flower border in microcosm.

Preparing Containers

Every container needs to be well prepared before you can begin to create your dried-flower arrangement. For containers with narrow tops, push a mound of chicken wire inside to support the stems. Otherwise, wherever possible, use dry green styrafoam. Fix the foam to the bottom of the container and then cover it with dry moss so that it cannot be seen when the arrangement is completed. It is a good idea to allow the moss-covered foam to stand proud of the container if you intend the flowers to hang over the sides, as this will lend extra stability to the arrangement.

Preparing baskets

You will need styraform, a knife, medium-gauge florist wire, adhesive tape and sphagnum moss.
1 *Indent a styrafoam block with base of the basket.*

2 *Cut the block to fit snugly inside the basket. Cut a second block to sit on top and form a mound 2.5cm (1in) above the basket rim. Make a needle out of the florist wire by turning one end back on itself to form an "eye".*

3 *Thread the adhesive tape through the eye and pass the needle through the top of the basket rim. Pull enough tape through to cover the width of the basket, allowing an extra 15cm (6in) to secure the ends.*

4 *Cut the tape and turn 7.5cm (3in) back on itself and around the cane to secure. Pull the tape across the dry foam and thread through the opposite rim. Secure the tape as before. Cover with dry sphagnum moss.*

Preparing deep bowls

Stick a plastic prong to the bottom of the bowl with adhesive clay. Cut a block of styrafoam to fit tightly inside the bowl and fix it firmly on the prong.

Preparing shallow bowls

Shape two blocks of styrafoam so that they form a mound over the rim of the bowl. Bind together with adhesive tape and glue the underside. Affix to the bowl.

Preparing glass containers

Stick two plastic prongs to the bottom of the container with adhesive clay and fix blocks of foam to them. The foam should sit 12mm ($\frac{1}{2}$in) short of the sides and 5cm (2in) short of the top. Poke pot-pourri or moss around the sides and on top with florist wires.

Arrangement Shapes

Arrangements in containers can take many different shapes. They can be short and squat, tall and narrow, perfectly semi-spherical, lop-sided, well-rounded or flat-backed to name just a few. However, although the range of shapes you can create might appear to be huge they are mostly related to the shape of a fan.

The shape of a fan can be applied to the curve the arrangement makes when seen from the front and from the side. The dimensions of the curves should be in proportion to each other and relate to the shape of the container. For example, when seen from the front, the sweep of the curve of an arrangement in an oval container should be broader than the curve seen from the side: in other words, the width of the arrangement should always be greater than the depth.

It is useful when creating an arrangement in a container to keep the fan shape in mind, but it is important not to follow the shape too rigidly. Look at the way plants grow in the garden. Many shrubs grow naturally into a roughly domed fan shape, but they are rarely perfect. It is also helpful to think of the container as the place from which the arrangement grows. So, in the simplest of all-round arrangements, the stems of the plant material should seem to spring from the center of the container in a natural and lively manner.

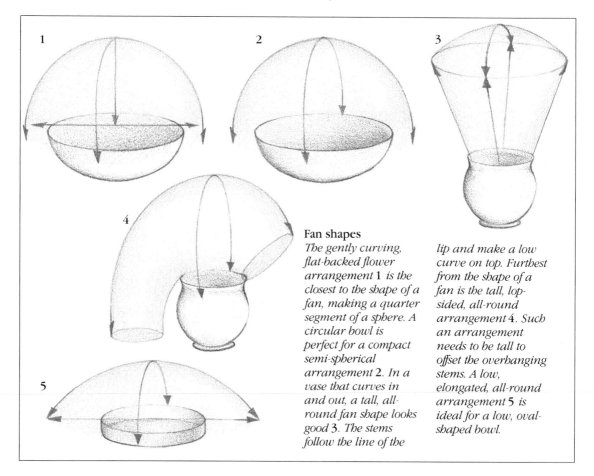

Fan shapes

The gently curving, flat-backed flower arrangement 1 is the closest to the shape of a fan, making a quarter segment of a sphere. A circular bowl is perfect for a compact semi-spherical arrangement 2. In a vase that curves in and out, a tall, all-round fan shape looks good 3. The stems follow the line of the lip and make a low curve on top. Furthest from the shape of a fan is the tall, lop-sided, all-round arrangement 4. Such an arrangement needs to be tall to offset the overhanging stems. A low, elongated, all-round arrangement 5 is ideal for a low, oval-shaped bowl.

Making a flat-backed arrangement

1 *Standing in front of the container, outline the flat, fan-shaped back of the arrangement with stems of meadowsweet. The central stem – the highest point – should measure twice the height of the container.*

2 *Make a quarter circle curve from the center back to the front of the arrangement. Following the angle of this curve, fill in the quarter segments with more meadowsweet to create a half-dome shape.*

3 *Now fill out the dome shape, roughly keeping to the curves of the basic arrangement. First add pink larkspur, then white statice, making sure that the two flowers are evenly distributed.*

4 *Still following the curves of the arrangement, add pink roses complete with foliage and wired hydrangea florets (see p.14) to make a full but airy, flat-backed, fan-shaped arrangement.*

Tall summer basket
This colorful, tall, half-open, fan-shaped arrangement is composed of larkspur, achillea, helipterum, helichrysum, miniature roses, myrtle, eryngium, poppy seed-heads and leucodendron foliage.

Elegant arrangement
Hydrangea, larkspur, statice, gypsophila, achillea and senecio foliage form this airy and delicate, tall, flat-backed, fan-shaped arrangement (above), which takes its colors from the mother-of-pearl vase.

Compact arrangement
This low, all-round, soft pink arrangement (left) of dahlias, statice, helichrysum, hydrangea, larkspur buds and anigozanthos is ideal for the squat, gently curving basket.

23

Dried-flower Trees

Nature is the most helpful guide when making a dried-flower tree and it is best to have a good look at living trees before deciding on the sort of shape that you would like to create. Some have dome-shaped heads and look rather like umbrellas, while others, like many conifers, have pyramid-shaped heads.

Once you have decided on the shape and size of the tree you wish to create you must decide on the container. The choice of container is very important and for the best effect you should select one large enough to create the impression that the dried-flower tree might actually be growing from it.

Making a dried-flower tree

You need a clay pot, styraform, a knife, plaster-of-Paris powder, water, a spoon, a miniature trunk, a styrafoam cone, short thin-gauge florist wires, dry sphagnum moss, alchemilla, red roses, wired celosia and twigs.
1 Line the pot with angled slices of dry styrafoam.

2 Mix the plaster-of-Paris powder with water. Quickly spoon the mixture into the pot until it is two-thirds full. Insert the miniature trunk in the center of the pot and, holding the trunk with one hand, spoon in the plaster to within 12mm ($\frac{1}{2}$in) of the rim.

3 Press a styrafoam cone on to the trunk. Bend the florist wires in half and pin clumps of sphagnum moss to the cone. Push the flower stems through the moss and into the cone, beginning with the alchemilla, then the roses, wired celosia and twigs until the cone is completely covered.

Tree shapes
Let nature be your guide when making a dried-flower tree unless you especially want to create an ornamental shape.

Mop-headed tree and copse
*Deep red helichrysum flowers and
pieces of purple* Celosia cristata
*make this a striking, mop-headed,
thick-trunked tree (above).
A foam lozenge covered in
golden rod impaled on several
birch twigs create this copse (left).*

Arrangements with Bases

Many types of arrangement do not need to be set in a container but require some sort of framework on which to be made.

Circular arrangements

A circular arrangement such as a wreath can be based on either a copper-wire frame, purchased ready-made from a flower shop or garden center, or a chicken-wire frame constructed by yourself. Alternatively, you can twist stems of woody vines, clematis, honeysuckle or grape, or supple twigs such as birch or willow, into a circle, entwining them and working in the ends so that the finished framework is firm enough to be used as a base for attaching a variety of dried flowers, should you wish. In fact, if carefully done, such a stem wreath can look beautiful in its own right (see p.29).

Dried-flower ropes

Another type of dried-flower arrangement that does not require a container is the dried-flower rope. Whether a small, delicate affair measuring just a few inches long, such as a circlet for a bride's headdress, or a long garland of flowers made to festoon a fireplace, table, archway or door, or to entwine the banisters or balustrade, or perhaps even to encircle the poles of a tented marquee, all dried-flower ropes are made using the same technique, although the bases vary in strength, type and thickness.

More delicate flower ropes like the circlet for the headdress are usually made on a wire base. Small bunches of flowers and foliage are attached to a piece of mossing (spool) wire, each overlapping the last. For a longer, more dramatic garland the bunches of dried flowers are fixed to

This informal, twisted birch twig and catkin wreath glows with rust and cream leucodendron cones.

stronger, plastic-coated garden wire, and even more substantial swagging is based on a framework of chicken wire stuffed with moss. Such a base can be as thick as you like and, indeed, any shape that you wish, too.

Wire-based ropes of dried flowers are certainly not the easiest arrangements to make, but they are well worth the trouble. Moreover, as you are working with dried flowers, you can prepare them in advance of the special occasion for which you have made them, thus avoiding the pressure of intricate, last-minute work that making fresh-flower garlands involves.

Dried-flower spheres

Chicken wire is very easy to mold and can be used to create the base for many differently shaped arrangements. A sphere shape is probably the most straightforward to make. You simply pile pieces of styrafoam, or clumps of hay or moss, on a strip of chicken wire then draw up the wire into a spherical shape, working the mesh around until the foam is firmly contained within it. The sphere can then be covered with damp moss to disguise the wire framework and allowed to dry out completely before fixing the dried flowers in it. A dried-flower sphere can be used to form the top of a tree, by spearing it on to a miniature trunk, or it can be used as an arrangement in its own right and suspended from the center of the ceiling.

More complicated base shapes can also be made using chicken wire. Each of the April Fools' Day rabbits on pages 76 and 77 are composed of several shapes formed out of chicken wire, stuffed with hay and joined together with spool mossing wire.

Circular Arrangements

There are several different methods of making bases for circular arrangements. The simplest method is to bind clumps of moss to a shop-bought wire frame, using string. Alternatively, you can weave supple stems together to form a circular frame, or roll chicken wire around sphagnum moss to form a long sausage and sew the ends together to make a circle. Chicken wire is very useful for dried-flower arrangers: it is also used for the base of a dried-flower sphere or a thick flower rope. For a delicate circlet of dried flowers florist wire is all you need for a base.

Making a wire-frame-and-moss base

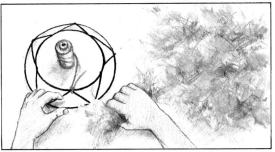

You will need a wire frame, a spool of string, some damp sphagnum moss and a pair of scissors.
1 *Tie the string to the frame, leaving a short length beyond the knot. Place some moss below the tie.*

2 *Bind the clump of moss to the frame. Wind the string firmly around frame and moss with one hand, while holding the moss in place with the other. The moss should be about 2.5cm (1in) thick on all sides.*

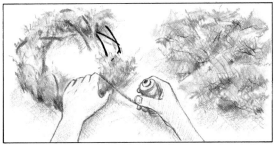

3 *Continue to bind in clumps of moss, maintaining a constant thickness and overlapping each clump. Overlap the last clump with the first. Cut the string and tie it to the short end beyond the joining knot.*

Making a chicken-wire-and-moss base

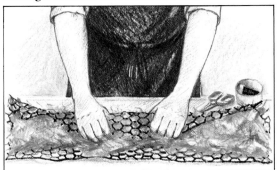

You will need chicken wire 30cm (1ft) wide, scissors, damp sphagnum moss and spool wire.
1 *Cut the chicken wire to the length of the circumference of the base you require. Lay the sphagnum moss along it and roll the wire over the moss to form a sausage shape 3.5cm (1½in) thick.*

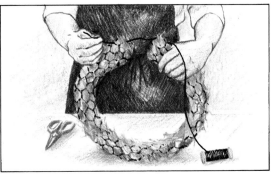

2 *Tuck in any protruding sphagnum moss and bend over sharp pieces of chicken wire at the ends. Bend the sausage shape gently to form a smooth circle. Tie the end of the spool wire to one end of the chicken wire and sew the two ends of the tube together. Cut the spool wire and secure the end.*

Making a stem base

You will need *supple stems, a pair of pliers, spool wire and a pair of scissors.*
1 Cut the stems into lengths of 1.3m (4½ft). Bend one stem length into a circle, overlapping the ends.

2 Bind the ends together with spool wire. Twist another stem length around the first and secure. Continue winding in lengths of stem until you achieve the thickness you require.

Making a delicate circlet

1 Join two florist wires and twist a loop at one end. Trim to 5cm (2in) longer than required and cover with floral tape. Bind on bunches with spool wire.

2 When 2.5cm (1in) from the end of the florist wire, bend to form a hook and ease the flower rope into a circle. Hook the wire through the loop to secure.

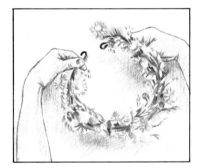

Making a moss-covered sphere

You will need *chicken wire 30cm (1ft) wide, a pair of scissors, styrafoam, spool wire and dry moss.*
1 Cut the chicken wire a little longer than the planned circumference of the sphere. Pile slices of styrafoam in the middle of the wire, and lift and bind the chicken wire into a sphere around the foam.

2 Tie the end of the spool wire to the chicken wire, leaving a short end for finishing. Place a clump of moss beside the knot and wind the spool wire around the sphere and moss. Bind on clumps of moss until the sphere is covered, then tie the spool wire to the short end and trim.

Eye-catching wreath
*A chicken-wire-and-moss base
with a froth of* Alchemilla mollis
(below) proves the perfect foil for
Carlina acaulis *'Caulescens'*
and Rosa *'Silva'.*

Decorated twig circle
*An actinidia twig base
shows through bunches
of dill, nigella seed-heads
and* Helichrysum
angustifolium *(above).
A plaited raffia
rope is entwined
in order to hang
the wreath.*

Circlets
*A mossed wire base is
covered in achillea
flower-heads, pompon
dahlias and loose knots
of raffia (far left). Behind
sits an evenly wound
vine wreath, attractive
without decoration.*

Hanging Arrangements

Dried-flower garlands, ropes and hanging bunches can transform a room or stairwell and are ideal when decorating the house for a special occasion. Sturdy, chain-link garlands made on a wire-and-hay base are ideal for hanging along a wall. Plaited ropes decorated with bunches of wired flowers and ribbon make an extremely attractive feature either side of the fireplace or along ceiling beams. More delicate garlands made with spool wire can be hung around doors and pictures and also look lovely adorning the banisters. A striking combination of bunches when wired together to make a globe shape and hung from the ceiling makes a truly grand centerpiece.

Making a chain-link garland

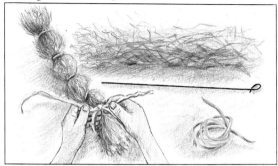

You will need heavy-gauge florist wire, some hay, raffia and your selected flowers.
1 *Loop the wire at one end to make an "eye". Cover the florist wire with hay and bind with raffia at intervals of 7.5cm (3in) to secure.*

2 *Bend the hay-covered wire into a circle. Thread the end of the wire into the loop and twist. Tidy the ends and conceal the join with a raffia tie.*

3 *Decorate the circlet with dried flowers. Form another link, decorate and thread through the first link. Continue until you have completed the chain.*

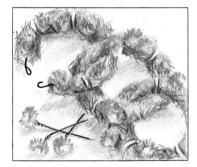

Making a plaited rope
You will need raffia, florist wire, some blue hydrangea flowers and yellow Helichrysum italicum.
1 *Take a good bunch of raffia strands and attach at the top to a firm support. Divide the raffia into three equal portions and weave the left portion and then the right portion alternately over the center portion until you reach the bottom of the strands.*

2 *Bind the ends firmly with raffia. Wire several small bunches of hydrangeas and helichrysum (see p.14). Insert the wire of the first bunch into the raffia at the top of the plait and bend back. Add the rest of the bunches in the same way.*

Making a spool-wire garland

You will need *spool wire, scissors, hydrangea florets, roses, oats and gypsophila.*

1 Make a loop in the spool wire at the point where the garland will end. Wire the hydrangea florets and small bunches of gypsophila (see p.14). Make a posy with all the ingredients and trim the stems.

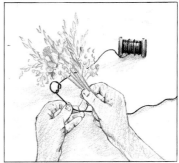

2 Hold the wire just below the loop and position the posy over it, so that the loop is completely covered with flowers. The garland will hang from this loop when it is finished.

Making a hanging globe

You will need *a 3.5cm (1½in) diameter curtain ring, florist wires, scissors, red bottlebrush, pink helichrysum, pink and yellow roses, green amaranthus, bupleurum, sea lavender and Leucodendron meridianum.*

3 Bind the posy to the wire with the attached spool wire. Continue binding on posies the length of the garland, overlapping the stems.

Making a spool-wire rope

1 Hang the curtain ring at a good working height or place in its final position. Wire separate bunches of each ingredient and then wire each bunch to the ring.

2 Continue to attach wired bunches of ingredients to the curtain ring until it is full. Finally, if not already in place, lift the globe to its hanging position.

For a wispy-looking rope, bind posies to spool wire in the same way as above but using material with longer stems.

Autumn rope
Leaves of beech, oak and fern are arranged into a circular, chicken-wire pad filled with moss (left). Fir cone twigs, helichrysum and gypsophila lie between the leaves and trail into a raffia plait that hangs from the center of the pad.

Delicate garland

Small bunches of ammobium, helichrysum, gypsophila and leptospermum together with clumps of Spanish moss, are wired on to a length of rope to create a delicate garland (below).

Robust swag

Bunches of fir cone twigs, pieces of osmunda fern, broom and Protea nerifolia *flowers are bound on to a length of mossing wire with spool wire (below).*

Design Guidelines

Nature is the best guide when creating arrangements of either fresh or dried flowers. There are no hard and fast rules. No two rose bushes look alike, no two oak trees are identical. In the same way, no two arrangements using the same ingredients will look exactly alike and, indeed, it is easy to make them look very different, even if they are created in identical containers.

Considering the location

Before choosing your plant material or container, or deciding on the shape of the arrangement, it is best to consider the position the arrangement will take. How large does it need to be? Will it be seen from all sides or will it stand against a wall? What sort of background will it be seen against: wallpaper? curtain material? Will it stand on a patterned carpet or rug? All these elements should affect your choice of flowers – their colors and textures – and container, and also the style of arrangement that you create.

Following nature

Allow your garden, or someone else's garden that you especially admire, to give you ideas for your arrangements. Look at the countryside: notice the shapes of the trees, and the way that plants and flowers grow into each other. Mostly, nature produces plant shapes that are well balanced and attractive when viewed singly or in groups. These are the shapes and groupings that you should bear in mind when creating your dried-flower arrangements.

Balance is important in an arrangement. An arrangement should never look as though it will fall over, never look uncomfortably crammed with flowers and never contain flower-heads that are much too large in proportion to the container. If in doubt, try it – you can always take them out and start again.

The importance of the container

The container is just as important to the arrangement as the flowers. Natural and simple containers are the most suitable for dried-flower arrangements. Baskets are particularly well suited, because they are actually made from dried material. Often the shape and texture of the basket will suggest shapes and textures for the arrangement. So, too, with other types of container. The design on a ceramic vase may well inspire the design of an arrangement, perhaps just because of its colors, or perhaps due to its shape and form. Dried flowers with warm, glowing colors look sumptuous in copper, brass and terracotta containers, while cool white and pale colored flowers look well in silver and stone containers.

Exciting colors and textures form this simple, scented arrangement in a bark container.

Bold mixture
This rustic primrose basket contains Erica arborea *and* E. carnea, Echinops ritro, *some skeletonized leaves and red fungi: a bold mix of shapes and textures.*

Color

So much plant material can be preserved that the color palette available to the dried-flower arranger is spectacular: bright reds, fresh greens, a wonderful range of pinks, clear yellows, hot oranges, cool creams, whites and silvers, lilacs and lavenders, purples and violets, and deep and pale blues. In fact, all the colors of the spectrum are represented and can be used in an infinite number of combinations to create a wide range of different effects.

Combining colors

It is a good idea to experiment with different combinations of colors in different quantities, when beginning to create dried-flower arrangements, to discover which colors look best together. In this way, your eye will soon become attuned to the effect colors have on one another when combined.

In general, colors that lie near each other in the spectrum blend together to create a subdued but none-the-less attractive combination. So, red and orange blend well, likewise orange and yellow, yellow and green, green and blue, and blue and violet. Colors at one remove from each other in the spectrum also combine well, but produce a more striking result. Red contrasts pleasantly with yellow, orange with green, yellow with blue and green with violet.

In essence, the further apart two colors are from one another the more startling the effect they create. Consequently, combinations of red and green flowers, red and blue flowers, and orange or yellow and violet or purple flowers will create an extremely dramatic effect. In addition, a strange visual effect is created when one color is combined in a small quantity with a larger amount of an opposing color. For example, a green arrangement appears even greener when a small amount of bright red is added. Similarly, a small quantity of bright yellow flowers amongst a mass of violet flowers intensifies the violet nature of the arrangement.

Tones and shades

Pastel colors are simply muted tones of primary and secondary colors. If you were creating a pastel color with paint you would add white, the color of light, to the primary or secondary color. Pale pink, peach and apricot, lilac, lemon and pale icy blues are all pastel colors. By adding black, the color of darkness, to a primary or secondary color you would create a more somber tone, such as brown, rust, gray, navy blue or plum.

Pastel tones and shades are especially well represented in dried flowers. There are a host of pink flowers, ranging from very bright to very pale, that are extremely easy to dry. Roses, larkspur, helipterum, statice, silene and helichrysum number among these. A smaller number of rust-colored flowers and leaves can be preserved: dock, statice, helichrysum, copper beech and hydrangeas fall into this color category. Only a few flowers that dry can be found in the peach and apricot range. They are: statice, roses, helichrysum and protea. Lavender, statice, hydrangeas, delphinium, amaranthus, cornflowers and dahlia all have lilac and plum-colored varieties.

Choosing colors

When deciding on the colors you want to feature in an arrangement, you should take into account the colors of the walls, carpets and furnishing fabrics in the room where the arrangement will be located. After that you will be dependent on your own taste to lead you to a color combination that will look good. By choosing colors that are close to each other in the spectrum you cannot really go wrong. On the other hand, you will probably create a more interesting and unusual arrangement by being a bit more adventurous in your choice of colors. Finally, consider the impact you wish to make. A large, centerpiece arrangement will probably require a dramatic use of color.

Blues and greens
The intense blues and greens of this matt-glazed earthenware vase provide the inspiration for an arrangement of pressed, green beech leaves, delphinium flower spikes in shades of blue, and clusters of sea holly.

Reds and yellows

An inlaid silver box with a daisy design is mounded with bright pink helipterum, and Senecio greyi *foliage and flower buds. The lining of the box is arranged with brilliant yellow helipterum that echo the color of the centers of the pink daisy flowers and relate the two daisy arrangements.*

Texture

The configurations of the surfaces of plant material and container dramatically affect the look of an arrangement. Dried plant material has many forms. There are the flowers themselves, ranging from the delicate, feathery quality of gypsophila and alchemilla to the large, dense flower-heads of peonies, roses, thistles and proteas. Seed-heads, too, such as poppies, love-in-a-mist, cereals and fir cones, all have strong shapes. Then there are the leaves, some sharp and pointed, some soft and rounded, some, like ferns, finely divided. They have smooth, flat surfaces, crinkly surfaces, indented and hairy surfaces. Think of the difference in texture between an ivy leaf and a lamb's ear, or *Stachys lanata*.

You can group these textural elements in an infinite number of ways to create an infinite number of different-looking arrangements.

Looking at individual plants

Each part of every plant has its own very special texture. Every petal of every flower produces areas of shade, defining its own texture. Take peonies and roses. At a glance they don't look very different. They both have many petals radiating from the top of the stem and their colors are frequently similar. Their textural differences are very small, yet on closer inspection you can immediately tell the difference between them. The outer petals of the rose bend outwards, while peony petals tend to curve inwards, and the inner petals of a peony are bunched in a less formal manner than those of a rose. The flower buds are in fact very different: peonies have rounded buds and roses more pointed buds. Their leaves, too, are quite dissimilar when viewed at close quarters.

Once you have learned to look carefully at plant material and can discern small textural differences between them it will come as second nature to consider the textures of dried material when creating an arrangement.

Combining textures

It is the combination of different shapes and textures that provides points of interest in an arrangement. Try positioning soft, rounded flowers against spires of spiky flowers; set groups of flowers against the solid forms of seed-heads and the defined shapes of leaves. Such contrasting combinations often work very well, creating arrangements with tangible textural presence.

A well-planned bed of plants contains a wide range of textures, providing fascinating juxtapositions within the overall shape of a border. Follow nature when choosing material for a dried-flower arrangement. Look at the way plants grow. See how leaves on adjacent plants overlap each other and how seed-heads intersect with other flowers. Look at the way that leaves highlight the flowers lying between them.

You may choose to use only two elements in an arrangement and this can be very effective. However, if they are similar-sized and similar-colored roses and peonies then the result will not be very interesting. A much more fascinating combination would be a mixture of roses and larkspur: whorled circles against bobbly spires. Alternatively, peonies and helipterum would look well together: large, crinkly circles set against small circles with serrated edges.

The overall view

Containers have texture, too, and all bring their textural qualities to bear on the overall look of the arrangement. The rough, pitted surface of a stoneware pot, the gnarled surface of a basket made from bark or twigs, the textured patterns of woven stems in wickerwork, the grainy surface of wood, the sheen of metal, and the smooth shine of a glass or glazed pot: all will add to the textural quality of an arrangement. Container and plant material should always relate to each other and the overall view should never be forgotten.

Textural variety
A lively arrangement of flowers and foliage of many different textures brings to life this heavy, gnarled old oil jar bound with a twisted cane decoration. Round-leaved spires of eucalyptus together with delicate spikes of kochia, larkspur and fir twigs vie with poppy seed-heads, cream corymbs of Verticordia *sp. and the rounded flowers of helichrysum and roses.*

Rough and smooth combination

A smooth, clear glass cylinder is filled with highly textural seeds, seed-heads, pot-pourri, bark and moss. Separate portions of cinnamon, dried chestnuts, lentils, pasta, lavender, sunflower seeds and corn-on-the-cob are squeezed against the sides of the glass by moss, while fir cones, poppy seed-heads and love-in-a-mist seed-heads are arranged in segments on top.

Style

Every arrangement of flowers – whether a garland or a vase arrangement – contains a number of design elements which together create a certain style. The shape, color and texture of the arrangement, together with the container if there is one and the situation in which the arrangement is placed, combine to give a total "look" or style.

The informality of dried flowers

Dried flowers have a natural and informal style of their own and however formal a shape you create, the completed arrangement will always have a sense of informality about it. For, the natural style of the flowers should greatly influence the style of the arrangement.

It is often a good idea to emphasize the informal nature of dried flowers, and some of the most successful dried-flower arrangements are those that have the informality of a summer garden. Containers with a rustic feel to them work well with such arrangements precisely because they are close to the look of the plants themselves. Baskets of all types, wooden trugs and boxes, terracotta and stoneware bowls, ceramics with less sophisticated designs and finishes, all lend themselves to natural-looking, dried-flower arrangements.

Careful planning

Although a natural-looking arrangement might appear simple to achieve, it actually requires careful planning if it is not to look artificial. To begin with, it needs strength of line: curves must be strong and straight lines must be well defined. For the lines are the bones of the arrangement: they give the arrangement its essential shape. Whether created by the stems, the leaves or seed-heads, or even the flowers themselves, they should be made first and the shape filled out afterwards. In this way the arrangement will be much easier to complete without spoiling the shape.

Cultivating your own style

Each of us has our own sense of style. When we open a magazine or book, certain images, colors and shapes appeal to us and we should draw upon these images when creating a dried-flower arrangement.

It is a good idea to make a note of the plants and colors that appeal to you. When you visit a garden, notice the combinations of flowers and foliage, and the shapes of the trees and shrubs that you like best. Then you can grow some of these plants yourself for drying, or buy bunches of them ready dried if you are not lucky enough to have a garden, and use them to create many different arrangements for your home – all reflecting your own sense of style.

The style of the room

Fortunately, many dried-flower arrangements fit in with even the most striking interior designs. The strong shapes of flowers like yarrow, the soft haze of fluffy gypsophila, the stately seed-heads of poppies and bulrushes: all these look wonderful against both the steel and glass of a cool, modern room and the warm, mellow wood of an old country house.

However, each room does have its own particular style, which might dictate a certain type of arrangement. The kitchen, a utilitarian place, is the ideal room in which to hang bunches of dried flowers from the ceiling, where they will be out of the way and will not clutter up work and eating surfaces, but will still form an attractive arrangement.

In the living room there is usually more space for table arrangements (see pp.51–3). Where there is a fireplace, a grand arrangement of dried flowers will cover the empty grate very attractively throughout the summer months (see p.63). The bedroom generally has a softer style and so a gentler, prettier, perhaps more subdued, arrangement will probably be more in tune there (see pp.59–61).

Simplicity of line
This tall, veined, glass vase and dried artichoke head look as though they were made for each other. It is an unlikely combination and one that you might not have considered unless you had observed the way an artichoke grows – the gentle curve of its thick stem, the muted colors of its heavy head. Strength of line, perfect balance and subdued colors combine to imitate nature.

Country-style basket
*An olive twig basket
spills over with bunches
of larkspur, oats,
limonium, phaenocoma,
ixodia, cornflowers,
salvia, gypsophila,
nigella and beech leaves.
The flowers have been
carefully arranged to
look as though the
bunches have just been
picked and laid into the
basket.*

DECORATING
WITH
ARRANGEMENTS

A head of Hydrangea macrophylla *cradles* Dahlia
'Dedham' and Limonium sinuatum *flowers.*

*F*lowers make an extraordinary difference to a room. They bring all that is best about the countryside into your home. And whether they are placed in a kitchen, a living room or even a ballroom, they add a warmth that is truly welcoming.

An arrangement of flowers reveals something about your taste, your color preferences, the shapes you like best and the textures you like to work with. For an arrangement is nothing less than a personal statement of creativity. This may sound rather alarming, but it isn't at all: we all have the ability to express ourselves creatively.

Our homes are one of the greatest statements about our taste. The colors, patterns, texture of walls, carpets, rugs, furnishing fabrics and the style of furniture we choose, combine to create an overall mood in a room or house. Dried-flower arrangements should, above all, reflect that mood. It is probably more important that a dried-flower arrangement fits in with its surroundings than a fresh-flower arrangement, as fresh flowers make a much more fleeting mark in a home. A dried-flower arrangement will be part of the furnishings for a year or more, until dust or sunlight removes the marvellous warm and mellow quality of the flowers.

So, before you begin arranging your dried flowers, consider carefully the wallpaper, paint, patterns, color of wood, shapes of furniture and the different textures that fill your room. Bear in mind the ornaments in the room, especially those that will sit near your arrangement. Take into account their scale and the dimensions of the surface that they and your arrangement will sit on. Then, and only then, choose your dried flowers and the container, making sure that they relate to all the elements.

Cottage Living Room

The decor
Terracotta and pink walls, and cream curtains with delicate rust flowers comprise the two main decorative elements to consider.

Strictly speaking, a cottage is a farm worker's house, although today a country home to which town dwellers retreat at weekends is often referred to as a cottage. Even so, when people talk of a cottage-style interior, they are usually referring to one particular style, a style that takes its inspiration from the countryside. Flowery printed fabrics for upholstery and curtains, mellow wooden tables, wooden or stone floors and warm, patterned rugs and carpets are the main ingredients of a simple, country-style interior.

Dried flowers are extremely well suited to pretty, cottage-style rooms and, indeed, in addition to providing vegetables, the original cottage garden produced an abundance of flowers for drying. It could still do so today: see pp.110–133 for some planting ideas.

Striking arrangement
Bright red miniature roses and pale pink Silene pendula *are combined in a rustic-looking terracotta pot and saucer. They create a dramatic yet warm arrangement that both stands out against the wall and blends with the warm, honey-colored, wooden table. Small pieces of foam were fitted into the gulley between pot and saucer and covered with crumbled rose leaves so that flowers could be arranged around the pot base.*

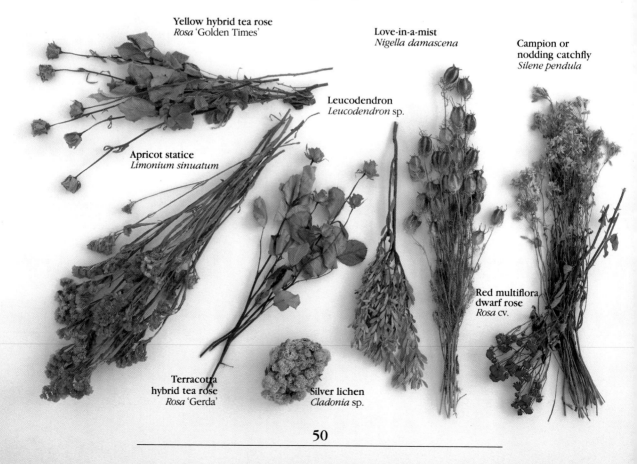

Yellow hybrid tea rose
Rosa 'Golden Times'

Love-in-a-mist
Nigella damascena

Campion or nodding catchfly
Silene pendula

Leucodendron
Leucodendron sp.

Apricot statice
Limonium sinuatum

Red multiflora dwarf rose
Rosa cv.

Terracotta hybrid tea rose
Rosa 'Gerda'

Silver lichen
Cladonia sp.

Subdued arrangement
A two-toned woven willow basket is ideal for this subdued arrangement that blends subtly with the wall color and table (left). The basic low dome shape was created with stems of leucodendron. Pinky-apricot statice and small wired bunches of love-in-a-mist seed-heads were then added to create the basic color scheme (below). A scattering of terracotta and yellow roses and some clumps of wired silver lichen "fill out" the arrangement.

Farmhouse Attic

Dried flowers and mellow rustic interiors are made for each other. Low, beamed ceilings, rough-cast walls and floors of untreated wood all relate so well to dried plant material that almost any choice of colors looks absolutely right. However, the proportions of the room will restrict the kind of dried-flower arrangement you can create. In an attic the ceiling will probably be low, so a table arrangement must not be too tall or it will look squashed. If you wish to make a tall arrangement it may well be better to stand it on the floor.

The warm colors of old tapestries are particularly suited to this type of room, where old Persian rugs and friendly, comfortable furniture always make one feel welcome and at ease. Use natural containers, such as baskets, terracotta pots or, if you are lucky enough to own one, a stone bowl or old wooden chest or box, for such a room and allow yourself to be influenced by both the overall mellow atmosphere and the decorative detail of the room. The pattern on a rug or curtain material will often suggest certain ingredients for an arrangement, or lead you to create a particular arrangement shape. The pressed fern and helichrysum in the arrangement at right echo the fern and daisy motifs featured in the paper lining of the box.

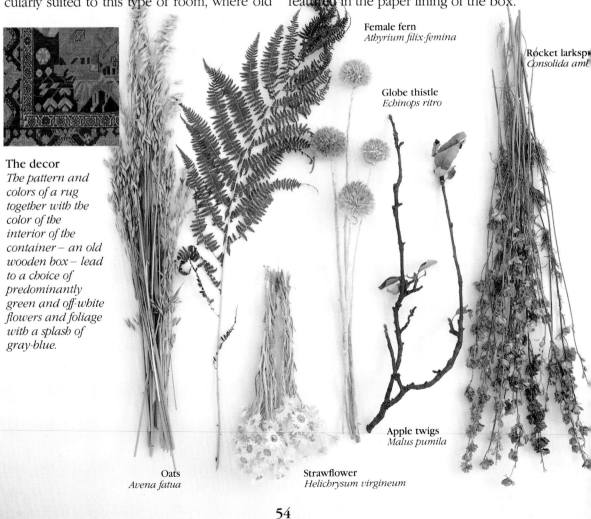

The decor
The pattern and colors of a rug together with the color of the interior of the container – an old wooden box – lead to a choice of predominantly green and off-white flowers and foliage with a splash of gray-blue.

Female fern
Athyrium filix-femina

Rocket larkspur
Consolida amb

Globe thistle
Echinops ritro

Apple twigs
Malus pumila

Oats
Avena fatua

Strawflower
Helichrysum virgineum

Informal arrangement
The painted paper lining of this eighteenth-century box is so beautiful that a section is left showing. The ingredients are arranged informally to accentuate the natural, relaxed atmosphere of the room.

Simple arrangement
Gnarled apple branches make a simple yet dramatic arrangement when set against the plain, light-colored wall of the attic room.

Romantic Bedroom

The decor
Delicately textured, soft pink wallpaper and matching pastel fabric set the scene.

Soft, gentle pastel colors are ideal for bedrooms. Creams, pinks, lilacs, *eau-de-Nil*, pale blues and greens all lend a soothing quality to a room and will help create a bedroom that feels warm but not too hot in winter and cool but not too cold in summer. Soft lines created by draping material over furniture so that it hangs in curves and folds will add to the relaxing atmosphere, and the delicate texture of a simple bowl of dried flowers, summer-grown in the garden, will look perfect in such a setting. Such an arrangement will also provide a joyful reminder of lazy, sunshine-filled days – something of a myth, perhaps, but nevertheless a great comfort.

Summery arrangement
The gentle curve of the blue ceramic bowl with a low, domed, pretty arrangement of wistful summery flowers contrasts with the tall elegance of the silver candlestick lamp and stands out against the pastel-colored wall.

Hybrid tea rose
Rosa 'Bridal Pink'

Sphagnum moss
Sphagnum sp.

Larkspur
Consolida ambigua

Hydrangea
Hydrangea macrophylla 'Hortensia'

Royal fern
Osmunda regalis

Lily
Lilium auratum rubrum

Perennial delphinium
Delphinium elatum

Common immortelle
Xeranthemum annuum

Small-headed yarrow
Achillea ageratum

Hybrid tea rose
Rosa 'Darling'

Rich pink everlasting
Helichrysum bracteatum

Globe thistle
Echinops ritro

Pink everlasting
Helichrysum bracteatum

Swan River everlasting
Helipterum manglesii

Tansy
Chrysanthemum vulgare

Purple statice
Limonium sinuatum

Love-in-a-mist
Nigella damascena

Senecio
Senecio greyi

Silver-leaved everlasting
Helichrysum augustifolium

Delicate arrangement
*This delicate trifoliate china dish
holds a sea of pale blue
delphinium flowers. Sand-dried
pink roses and an auratum lily
float nonchalantly on top.*

Period Dining Room

The decor
Rich sunny yellow provides the backdrop.

The formal dining room is used mostly in the evenings and the decorations should therefore take into account that they will frequently be seen under artificial light. Consequently, it can be a good idea to embrace fairly strong color themes, such as warm, golden yellows, refined, austere grays, or sunny, Mediterranean terracottas. The furniture is usually solid, creating strong shapes. Dining table and chairs, sideboard and perhaps a fireplace need to be set off with bold dried-flower arrangements. In summer a grand arrangement can transfigure an empty fireplace and in winter the mantelshelf or sideboard make ideal locations for smaller arrangements.

Yellow arrangement
Inspired by the strong wall color, a striking basket arrangement with an abundance of yellow flowers fills the elegant fireplace throughout the summer.

Silver poplar
Populus sp.

Large-headed centaurea
Centaurea macrocephala

White and blue larkspur
Consolida ambigua

Poppy
Papaver sp.

Cider gum
Eucalyptus gunnii

Golden yarrow
Achillea filipendulina 'Coronation Gold'

Summer cypress
Kochia sp.

Mimosa or wattle
Acacia sp.

Chinese lantern
Physalis alkekengi

Sunray
Helipterum cotula

Australian spider bush
Grevillea sp.

Lavender cotton
Santolina sp.

Lively arrangements
A Delft plate provides the inspiration for these lively mantelshelf arrangements.

Dramatic Studio Room

Intense blues, startling reds, rich oranges, sharp yellows and strong greens can all be used in striking combinations to decorate and furnish a room. However, it is no simple matter to devise a bold color scheme. In fact, if carelessly handled, striking colors can make a room extremely uncomfortable to live in. It is usually best to begin with an ornament or piece of furniture and build up a vibrant color scheme from that: a painting often provides the basis of a scheme for the whole room, with fabric, floor and wall colors all echoing the colors of the painting.

Many flowers retain their strong color when dried. This is especially the case with helichrysum and roses, which can therefore play a dramatic role in a vibrant room. Other less boldly colored dried flowers and well-shaped or textured foliage can act as a fascinating foil for vivid background colors.

Wild arrangement
A striking arrangement of large-leaved bamboo and hydrangea heads makes a very positive statement in this boldly decorated room.

The decor
The intense blue walls and bold abstract fabric design create the drama.

Mop-headed hydrangea
Hydrangea macrophylla

Japanese bamboo
*Pseudosasa
japonica*

Strawflower
*Helichrysum
bracteatum*

Cornflower
Centaurea cyanus

Leucodendron
Leucodendron sp.

**Cerise-tinged
hybrid tea rose**
Rosa 'Mercedes'

**Deep yellow
hybrid tea rose**
Rosa
'Golden Times'

**Scarlet-tinged
hybrid tea rose**
Rosa 'Jaguar'

Corn-on-the-cob
Zea mays

Statice
Limonium sinuatum

Strawflower
Helichrysum italicum

Leucodendron
Leucodendron sp.

Phaenocoma shrub
Phaenocoma prolifera

Pine
Pin

Dramatic circlet
*A wild circle of dried
flowers vies with the
brilliant colors of the
tea set and sofa fabric.*

ARRANGEMENTS FOR SPECIAL OCCASIONS

Feathery plumes of Alchemilla mollis *surround*
Helipterum manglesii *and waxy ixodia flowers.*

*L*ife would be very dull without special occasions. They give a shape and form to the year and afford us the chance to celebrate, which is what life should be all about. And wherever there is celebrating, there should be flowers.

Many people have parties on New Year's Day. After the celebrations of New Year's Eve, which keep most people up well beyond midnight, it is good to have a quieter celebration with friends and relatives. Twelfth Night and Valentine's Day follow in seemingly quick succession. Both of these are about casting off the old and beginning afresh: a new direction and a new love.

April Fools' Day is essentially a day (or morning) of fun, when even the media play jokes. Ridiculous items are delivered with a sincerity that often takes one in – for a moment, at least. Easter, the great Christian festival commemorating the resurrection of Christ, and, in earlier times, the beginning of the New Year, brings to an end the first cycle of days of celebrations. They begin again later in the year with harvest thanksgiving, and the biggest celebration of all – Christmas – completes the year.

In between, there are birthdays, weddings and christenings, all joyful occasions when flowers can mean so much, and some people do not allow Midsummer's Day to pass without celebration. If you are arranging only dried flowers for any of these occasions, you will have the advantage of time, for you can prepare such an arrangement well in advance of the day. This is invaluable if you know you will have hundreds of last minute things to organize.

Valentine's Day

How Valentine's Day came to be a festival for lovers is shrouded in mystery. Two martyrs, both called St Valentine, are recorded as having suffered persecution by the emperor Claudius, and both died on 14 February AD 270. However, the way we celebrate the day does not have anything to do with either of them!

Pagan festival

Valentine's Day as we know it may derive from the feast of Lupercalia, which was a pagan festival that took place in mid-February. Fertility rites were performed at this festival, including one in which boys drew the names of girls from a love urn. It may have been converted to a Christian festival by attaching it to the Saint's Day nearest to it, namely St Valentine's Day.

Valentine cards

The first Valentine cards date from the very beginning of the British postal system in the sixteenth century when elaborate lace paper cards were produced complete with verses. The more recent practice of leaving the missive unsigned adds a sense of playful mystery to the event. You could make your own Valentine card simply by writing your own verse on a piece of plain card and mounting a border of pressed flowers such as violets or primroses on to it.

Red roses

The red rose has long been a symbol of true love and is now associated with Valentine's Day. This is a more recent innovation, of course, as in colder climes roses are not in flower at this time of year and available only at great expense.

However, roses dry very well and red roses keep their intense rich color for many months if they are dried correctly (see p.94). Attaching a single bloom to a present makes an everlasting, poignant memento. Alternatively, an arrangement of dried flowers containing some red roses makes a loving present.

Valentine heart
*A heart of red roses
makes a very special
Valentine's Day present
in true Victorian style.*

Making a heart of red roses

You will need one 2.5cm (1in) diameter, moss-filled chicken-wire tube 1m 15cm (3ft 9in) long, two thin tubes, one 38cm (15in) and the other 10cm (4in) long, mossing wire, silver-sprayed tree heather, small-headed sedge, and eighty red roses with stems cut to a length of 3.5cm (1½in).

1 Bend the large tube into a heart shape and join at the top with mossing wire. Bind on sprays of silver heather, overlapping the sprays to cover the entire frame.

2 Take the 38cm (15in) tube and set the 10cm (4in) tube at right angles to one end. Bind it on with mossing wire to make a "T" shape. Bend to form a point.

3 Divide the sedge into small bunches of increasing stem lengths. Bind the shortest bunch to the top of the arrow-shaft with mossing wire.

4 Continue adding sedge until two-thirds of the way down the shaft. Bind two small bunches of sedge on either side of the arrow-head with raffia.

5 From the back, feed the shaft diagonally through the center of the heart until the head protrudes by 5–7.5cm (2–3in). Tie the shaft to the heart with mossing wire.

6 Bind the shaft just under the arrow-head to the bottom of the heart. Attach a silver ribbon or raffia bow to the arrow-shaft to cover the last wire tie.

7 Insert the stems of the roses, which should be cut at a razor-sharp angle, into the heart. Check they are firmly in position and cut off any protruding stems.

April Fools' Day

Sometimes called All Fools' Day, the first day of April is a day for playing practical jokes on friends and neighbors. No one is quite sure where or how this ancient tradition originated. One possible explanation dates back to Roman times. At the beginning of April the Romans celebrated the festival of Cerealia, which had its origins in the following story. While picking flowers in the Elysian meadows, Proserpina, the daughter of Ceres, was whisked away by Pluto to the lower world. Ceres went in search of Proserpina but, although she could hear the screams of her daughter, she was never able to find her, for the screams were only echoes – she had been sent on a fool's errand.

Customary terms

In France an April Fool is known as a *Poisson d'Avril* or an April Fish. This may be because the zodiacal sign of Pisces comes to an end shortly before the beginning of April. Alternatively, the term may have arisen because in April fish are stupid simply because they are very young: they are therefore easily caught. Whichever theory is true, the custom is the same: to make a friend, neighbor or relative look slightly foolish.

In Scotland "hunting the gowk" has long taken place on April Fools' Day. A gowk is a cuckoo, commonly thought of as a stupid bird, and an April Fool is known as an April Gowk.

April Fools' Day jokes

In Europe the most likely explanation of April Fools' Day is that the festival is related to the celebration of the Old New Year. The Old New Year began on 25th March and festivities lasted a week, ending on 1st April. In the sixteenth century the date of the New Year was altered to 1st January and consequently the tradition of giving presents to welcome the New Year was also altered. Possibly people were annoyed by the setting up of the new calendar and decided that they would continue to give presents on 1st April, but that they would have a jokey quality.

In recent times the BBC has broadcast jokey items of information as part of the news on April Fools' Day. A notable April Fools' Day story broadcast about twenty years ago concerned the surprisingly early harvesting of spaghetti from the spaghetti trees in Italy. To accompany the story the BBC showed a film of bunches of spaghetti being gathered from the trees. It seems incredible that viewers could be taken in by such a story, but it was very convincingly set up and people were much less widely travelled then.

It is always great fun to set up a practical joke especially for the children in the family. You might like to make a rabbit or other cuddly animal using a chicken-wire frame and moss, and surprise them at breakfast time.

This cheerful little bunny is formed out of chicken wire and is not difficult to make (see p.77).

Friendly mossy rabbits
These natural-looking mossy rabbits would look very convincing placed in the garden on April Fools' Day morning.

Making a mossy rabbit
You will need *chicken wire, hay, fresh silver lichen and spool mossing wire.*
1 *Bend the chicken wire into the shape of the head and body of the rabbit. Form individual legs and a tail out of smaller pieces. Attach to the body with spool wire.*

2 *Fill the head, body, legs and tail with hay. Tie the spool wire to the frame and bind on clumps of lichen to the body, overlapping each clump and winding the spool wire tightly round the frame to hold it in place. Cover the head, legs and tail in exactly the same way.*

Easter

The word Easter is derived from the name of the Anglo-Saxon goddess of spring, *Eostre* or *Ostara*, and has always been connected with April, or *Eostre monath*.

Christians have celebrated Easter on various dates during or close to April since the early days of the Church. Although commemorating the resurrection of Jesus Christ, the festival itself is not mentioned in the New Testament. The early Christians continued to celebrate Jewish festivals and the Passover (in Hebrew, *pesach*) with Christ as the Paschal Lamb became the Christian Easter festival. In many countries the festival name is derived from the Latin *Pascha* and the French, Italian, Spanish and Dutch names are all very similar to the Latin. Constantine decreed that Easter, the most important festival of the Christian year, should also be the first day of the New Year and this continued to be the case until the sixteenth century when the date of the New Year was moved to 1st January, giving rise to April Fools' Day (see p.75).

Fixing the date

Easter Sunday is the first Sunday after the full moon following the vernal equinox, so the date varies from year to year and, strictly speaking, also from place to place. There were many arguments about this calculation and so it was that by AD 455 the Roman and Alexandrine celebrations of Easter were separated by as much as eight days.

With the Gregorian correction to the calendar in 1582, Easter Sunday, although still varying from year to year, was made to fall on the same day wherever you were in the world. However, the debate continues as to whether Easter Sunday should fall on the same day of the month every year. At present, Easter Sunday can be as early as the end of March or as late as the very last Sunday in April.

Easter eggs

The egg has long been a symbol not only of birth but of the coming of spring, so it is not surprising that the early Christians attached this pagan symbol to the festival that fell nearest to the spring festival of pagan times – Easter.

It was forbidden to eat eggs during Lent, so at Easter baskets of eggs were taken to the churches to be blessed and then consumed afterwards at a great feast. In the country, children would collect eggs from friends and neighbors at Easter. In the seventeenth century they began decorating the eggs with vegetable dyes.

In the northern hemisphere early spring flowers burst open at Easter. At the same time birds are nesting and fledglings hatching, so a nest of dried flowers and decorated eggs seems a most appropriate Easter decoration.

Hens' eggs can be decorated in all sorts of colorful ways using fast-drying paint.

An Easter nest
A chicken-wire frame covered in hay and twig bunches forms the nest. Inside, helichrysum, Limonium sinuatum, Silene pendula, Anigozanthos *sp. and* Pithocarpa corymbulosa *are fixed in hay-covered styrafoam, while decorated eggs nestle at the front.*

Hallowe'en

Hallowe'en, the evening before All Hallows' Day (1st November), has been observed since early times and has always had particularly spooky associations.

Pagan festival

Our ancestors thought that Hallowe'en was the night when evil spirits, witches, demons, ghosts and hobgoblins walked abroad, so they lit bonfires to ward off these sinister spirits. The Celts and Anglo-Saxons held a fire festival on All Hallows' Eve to protect their crops from the evil and dark spirits of the winter solstice, which begins in the early days of November. The Druids, too, lit bonfires to honor their sun god at this time of the year.

All Hallows' or All Saints' Day was instituted by Pope Boniface IV when he was trying to stamp out pagan rites and to ensure that the Pantheon in Rome, built as a temple to the ancient gods, was henceforth used as a Christian church for the Virgin Mary and all martyrs. However, we continue to celebrate the pagan tradition of Hallowe'en on 31st October to a much greater extent than the Christian festival of All Hallows' Day.

Traditional celebrations

The Scots light fires and hollow out turnips. They cut a face out of the turnip skin, place a lighted candle inside and call it a Jack o'Lantern. Americans began celebrating Hallowe'en in the late nineteenth century, using home-grown pumpkins instead of Scottish turnips. The British have now adopted the pumpkin, which has a wonderful glowing skin and is rather easier to carve out than a turnip.

It was the Americans who instituted the sport of trying to pick up an apple with your teeth while the apple was bobbing in a barrel of water. This game still takes place in many parts of America alongside the more recent game of trick or treat. This is the custom in which children, wearing fancy dress, demon masks and witches' cloaks, troop round all the houses in the neighborhood and demand of the person who opens the door: "Trick or treat?" Usually they are given a treat of sweets or cake but some more courageous householders choose to be subjected to a trick.

Harvest festival

The late harvest connotations of Hallowe'en celebrations make using dried plant material in decorations very appropriate. Gourds, wheat, oats, barley and corn-on-the-cob, as well as freshly hollowed out pumpkins (their color is lovely) or turnips can all be used to spooky effect. Simply place lighted candles or torches in the pumpkin heads and watch the shadows.

Hallowe'en party
Shadows make sinister ghostly shapes of the scarecrows (right), while lighted pumpkin faces grin mischievously. Colorful gourds (below) make an attractive feature.

Making a scarecrow
*You will need a
terracotta pot 35cm
(14in) in diameter, styrafoam, plaster-of-Paris, a
stake 1.3m (4ft 6in) tall
and 2.5cm (1in) square,
sphagnum moss or
lichen, mossing wire, a
besom or twig broom,
some hay, two bunches
of dried wheat, a piece of
wood 75cm (2ft 6in)
long and 12mm (½in)
square, some raffia and
a pumpkin.*

1 *Line the pot with styrafoam. Make a fairly thick
plaster-of-Paris mixture.
Place the stake in the
pot, pointed end up.
Spoon in plaster-of-Paris
until the pot is three-
quarters full. Cover with
sphagnum moss or lichen.*

2 *Lash the broom to the stake with
mossing (spool) wire. The top of the
broom handle should sit 13cm
(5in) below the top of the stake.*

3 *Bind on the shorter piece of
wood at right angles to the stake
on top of the broom. Bind bunches
of wheat stems to the broom twigs.*

4 *Cover the arms and body above
the skirt with hay and tie on with
raffia. Tie a plaited raffia belt at
the top of the skirt.*

5 *Scoop out the flesh of the
pumpkin and make the face.
Spear the head on to the stake
and place a small torch inside.*

Christmas

Christmas, or Christ's Mass, has been celebrated as the birth of Christ on 25th December since the early part of the fourth century. Before that the emperor Aurelian chose 25th December as the birthday of the unconquered sun and, to this day, Christmas contains elements of the winter rites linked with the solar calendar called the Kalends.

Christmas decorations
When we decorate houses with greenery and colored lights and exchange presents we are performing part of the ancient pagan rites. In fact, that most pagan of all plants, mistletoe, was allowed into the home and the Church only after Pope Gregory I agreed that pagan customs should be assimilated into the Christian ethic.

Prince Albert was responsible for making the Christmas tree popular in Britain when he imported a number from his estate in Coburg in 1845. Before that it played a part only in the German festivities.

Father Christmas
The figure of Father Christmas, Santa Claus or St Nicholas – all one and the same person – has been with us since the fourth century. St Nicholas was Bishop of Myra and a great philanthropist. A sporting fellow, one Christmas time he climbed on to a roof-top at night and dropped a bag of gold down the chimney. It fell into a stocking drying below and was found by an astonished man the next morning. Hence, our custom.

Dried flowers at Christmas
Dried flowers can be used in Christmas decorations to stunning effect either on their own or mixed with fresh greenery such as pine, yew and holly. Many varieties of conifer, such as blue pine, Scots pine and Irish yew, dry well. If you use dried flowers and conifer you can make your Advent wreaths, basket arrangements, garlands and even trees well in advance of Christmas in the knowledge that they will last throughout the whole of the festive season. If you wish to make some garlanding using dried material and holly, add the holly just before Christmas as both its leaves and berries will soon wilt in a warm room.

Christmas color
Brightly colored dried flowers, such as Chinese lantern, red helichrysum, red roses and bottlebrush, look dashing against the dark rich greens of Christmas trees and foliage. So, too, do the ice-cool whites, silvers and pale blues of gypsophila and larkspur, helichrysum, senecio and santolina foliage, and hydrangea and pale blue larkspur. Anything goes when you are decorating a tree and a great mixture of flowers and colors always looks wonderful. However, a tree decorated in one or two colors, perhaps red and green, pink and silver or orange and gold, can look as stunning as one bedecked with every color under the sun.

Silver baskets filled with dried lilac-blue hydrangea heads.

Christmas garlanding
Ropes of dried flowers and foliage will brighten the house during the Christmas season. Fireplaces, doorways and stair-cases, tables, shelves and pictures are given new life when surrounded by garlanding. Using rich green foliage provides an added brilliance, but ropes made entirely from dried material can also be stunning and you can make dried-flower ropes at your leisure, well before Christmas.

Making a garland

You will need long and short lengths of red and green raffia, Picea glauca *(silver spruce)*, red, orange, yellow and small pink helichrysum, Silene pendula *and bright red* Physalis alkekengi *(Chinese lantern)*. You can either buy ready-colored raffia or spray natural raffia with matt or glossy spray paint. If possible, buy long lengths of untreated raffia and place in an old cardboard box before spraying, preferably in the open air.

1 *Take some long pieces of green and red raffia and tie the ends together with a short length of raffia. You can cover the tie with a bow when the garlanding is in position. Pull apart ten or so strands of the raffia base. Tie on a small bunch of flowers or some greenery with a short length of raffia, making a bow to finish. Continue attaching bunches in this way down the length of the switch. The ingredients should lie in the same direction as the fall of the rope.*

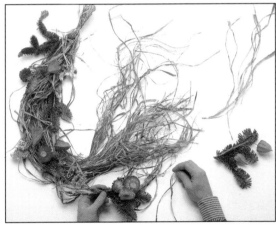

2 *Tie a fresh switch of raffia to the ends of about half of the first switch. Attach bunches in the same way as before. If you intend laying the garlanding over the top and down the sides of a picture or door, then you will need to alter the direction in which the ingredients lie in accordance with the direction of the garland. It is often a good idea in this case to work outwards from the center of the garland in each direction. Once the garland is in place you can manipulate flowers and foliage so they point the right way.*

Staircase decorations
The banister is decked with raffia garlanding (see p.84), which contains the same ingredients as the dried-flower tree (see p.86) standing on the staircase.

Making a dried-flower tree

You will need Chinese lanterns, orange, yellow and pale pink helichrysum, Silene pendula, *silver spruce 5–7.5cm (2–3in) long, silver lichen and dyed, dark green lichen, together with florist wires about 7.5cm (3in) long bent into hairpins to decorate this styrafoam-based tree.*

Starting from the top, layer the lichen moss on to the tree, mounded ends pointing towards the base and each clump overlappng the next. Use the two colors of moss randomly. Next add the spruce, then the remainder of the ingredients.

Christmas basket

Twirling tartan ribbons fly amongst contorted hazel twigs in this wild-looking arrangement. They spring from a blaze of scarlet and green painted poppy seed-heads and fresh spruce sprigs.

Cool, elegant tree (overleaf)
*Silver baskets filled with dried
hydrangea heads (see p.83), and
crisp, white, dried gypsophila
dusted with glitter adorn this
elegant tree.*

Birthday

Flowers have been a traditional birthday present around the world for centuries and it is difficult to think of a more beautiful gift. Fresh flowers are wonderful, of course, their very transience a part of their charm. However, dried flowers make a far superior gift, for while the blooms of fresh flowers will fall within a week or so, dried flowers will continue to look beautiful for a year or even longer.

Flowers and their meanings

Every flower has a special meaning, so when you give flowers as a present you give a message, too. Red and pink roses signify love; white roses, innocence; but steer clear of yellow roses as these signify jealousy. The poppy represents long life, while clematis signifies beauty of thought. The violet denotes faithfulness and rosemary, remembrance. All these plants can be dried and used in arrangements.

In addition, each of the signs of the zodiac is associated with a flower, and most of them can be dried. So why not make a gift of a bouquet or container arrangement of dried flowers, using only the type of flower associated with the recipient's star sign? Alternatively, use flowers of varying hues of the color linked to their star sign. In some cases you could do both! The flower for Aries is the anemone and the color is ruby red. Forget-me-nots and turquoise are linked with Taurus. Lily-of-the-valley and gray and yellow with Gemini; magnolias and white and sea green with Cancer; marigolds and orange with Leo; lavenders and gray and yellow with Virgo; lilies and pink and blue with Libra; orchids and ruby red with Scorpio; carnations and purple with Sagittarius; poppies and navy blue, black and

white with Capricorn; gentians and royal blue with Aquarius; and gardenias and aquamarine with the sign of Pisces.

Posies and bouquets

A birthday gift of dried flowers can take many different forms. The simplest arrangement to give is a delicate posy of flowers or a small bouquet (see p.16). A bunch tied with a pretty bow can look very attractive and, if you are growing flowers in your garden for drying, it is a good idea to hang up some mixed bunches of flowers, foliage and seed-heads at the drying stage, so that when they are dry you have some ready-made presents. You might add some attractive wrapping, or simply tie a bunch with a raffia or satin bow. If you want to create an arrangement that is a little more special, choose flowers and foliage that will suit the decor and furnishings of the recipient's house.

Scented gifts

Perfumed dried flowers in the form of pot-pourri make a present that will give a delicious scent to a room for many months. You could use pot-pourri at the base of a dried-flower arrangement. Or you could create an arrangement in a glass container and place a thin layer of scented petals into that small gap between the glass and the styrafoam. This way the container will look as though it is made of pot-pourri and the gift will be scented. Even a birthday card can involve dried flowers. Why not use hand-made textured paper and fix a group of pressed flowers like pansies and primroses or just a beautiful single flower or leaf on to the front? The flowers could be appropriate to the day.

A sumptuous birthday basket (see p.90) wrapped and ribboned.

Birthday basket
A woody basket, fragrant with pot-pourri, is filled with red roses, poppies, pink larkspur, Chinese lanterns, safflowers and Alchemilla mollis *to create a truly sumptuous present. Wrapping it in cellophane and adding red ribbons completes this wonderful gift (see p.89).*

DRYING AND PRESERVING TECHNIQUES

A beautiful creamy desiccant-dried peony with
Senecio greyi *foliage and flower buds.*

*T*here are several methods of drying and preserving plant material. Of the drying techniques, the easiest and most effective method is air drying. Simply leave the material in a cool, dry, shady place with good ventilation. Usually, it is best to hang the plant material upside-down, either in single stems or well-spread bunches. Harvest the material to be air dried in dry conditions about four days before the flowers reach perfection, or when foliage and seed-heads are mature: the quality of your result will depend very much on the quality of your raw material. Tidy up the plant material first and, if it is to be hung in bunches, remove the lower leaves where the tie will be.

You can also dry plant material by pressing it between weighted sheets of absorbent paper, such as blotting paper or newspaper. However, using this method results in two-dimensional plant material, ideal only for decorating flat surfaces. A more difficult drying method, which is, however, very effective in terms of retaining both color and form, is to use a desiccant. Place the plant material in a tin and pour silica gel, borax, alum or sand, or a combination of all these desiccants, around it. Seal the tin and allow the desiccant to draw out the moisture.

Plants and, in particular, foliage can also be preserved in glycerine. Simply set the material in a solution of glycerine and water: it will drink up the solution until it is saturated. Material preserved in this way will last for many months. What is more, the plant material will remain flexible and will therefore be easy to use. Crystallizing is an excellent method of preserving edible flowers and leaves. The delicious coating of sugary crystals makes them look and taste wonderful, especially when they cover a mouth-watering gâteau!

Air Drying

Air drying is the easiest and most effective method of preserving plant material and most of the plants used in the arrangements in this book have been air dried. Depending on the type of plant, the material can be dried hanging upside-down, standing upright in a container, or simply lying on the floor.

Ideally, plant material should be air dried in a room that is cool, dry, well-ventilated and dark, although you can air dry flowers in warmer temperatures and in a room or cupboard without a moving air current. However, it is imperative that the drying room is both dry and dark. If it is not dry, the plant material will rot, especially where the stems or flowers are touching, such as at the tying point of a hanging bunch. If the room is not dark, the flowers will fade extremely quickly.

Harvesting for air drying
All plant material should be picked in dry weather, preferably around or after midday, when any dew will have evaporated. Flowers should be picked approximately four days before they reach their prime. In other words, a rose should be picked when the bud is colorful and on the point of opening.

Hang drying
Hanging material to dry is the most common method of air drying. *Helichrysum bracteatum,* limonium, roses with the hybrid-tea-shaped flowers, all helipterum, rocket larkspur, Chinese lantern, hydrangea, achillea, *Ammobium alatum* and dahlias all dry best using this simple method.

Before hanging the material, remove all the lower leaves and wipe away any moisture on the stems with kitchen paper or a towel. Then tie the stems together into bunches with lengths of raffia or string, or even an elastic band. Make sure the stems beneath the tie are short enough to be able to hang the bunches upside-down in position. Fan out the flowers, seed-heads and leaves in each bunch so that there is as little contact between the leaves and petals as possible. Then attach the bunches or single stems upside-down to a rail, wire or length of string in your drying place. Hang the groups of bunches so that they do not touch one another: it is better to dry a few flowers well than dry many flowers so badly that you are presented with a disaster area of decay.

Check the flowers from time to time as they are drying. Different plants take different amounts of time to dry. Helichrysum and helipterum dry quite quickly – in about three weeks – roses take a little longer, while it is several months before the fleshy stems of sedum have lost all their moisture. Do not be tempted to take the flowers down before they are completely dry, or the stems will soon droop and the flowers disintegrate.

Drying upright
Some material air dries well when placed upright in a container. Gypsophila, hydrangeas and hybrid delphiniums dry particularly well when stood in a small amount of water that slowly evaporates, while grasses, rushes, cereals and many other seed-heads dry perfectly if left to stand in an empty vase. They can even be arranged just after picking and left to dry in position. As with hanging bunches, the material needs to stand in a cool, dry, well-ventilated, dark place for best results.

Drying flat
Some plant material can simply be laid on the floor or in a box to dry. Most deciduous and many evergreen leaves will dry in this way, although the leaves will develop crinkly edges. Mosses and cones can be laid in an airy box or basket to dry and you can sit larger heads of plants such as artichokes, big thistles, proteas or corn-on-the-cob on a chicken-wire shelf.

Wiring delicate flower-heads

You will need *a flower-head, florist wire, spool rose wire, scissors and floral tape.*

1 Hold the florist wire against the stem, with the tip touching the flower-head. Place the end of the rose wire at the end of the stem.

2 Bind the rose wire around the short end of rose wire, florist wire and stem. Continue for 7.5cm (3in), then cut.

3 Cover the extended stem with floral tape. Hold the wired flower-head upside-down and place the end of the tape just below the flower-head.

4 Wind the floral tape around the wired stem by twisting the wire so that the tape spirals up the extended stem. Continue just beyond the end of the wire, wind in and cut.

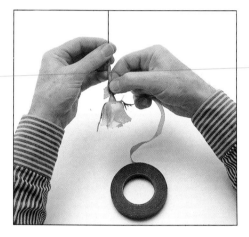

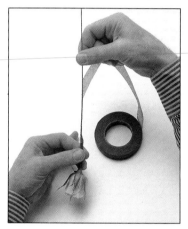

Wiring compact flower-heads

You will need *a flower-head or bud, florist wire and scissors.*

1 Cut the stalk 2.5cm (1in) below the flower-head. Cut the wire at a sharp angle, so you can easily push through the flower. Insert the wire into the hollow stem and push it through the flower-head, until it protrudes about 5cm (2in).

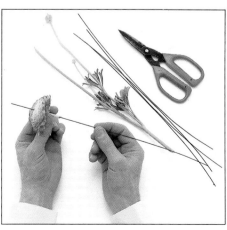

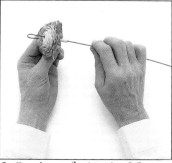

2 Bend over florist wire 2.5cm (1in) from the top. Pull the wire back so the open end of the "U" pierces the flower.

Bunching fresh stems

Bunching wired stems

You will need *fresh stemmed material, scissors and string or raffia.*
1 Cut away lower leaves and thorns where the tie will be.

2 Bind together loosely three or four stems, staggering the positions of the flower-heads. Make sure air can circulate around the heads so they dry without rotting.

Bind together about five wired stems with an elastic band. Bend the wires and stagger the flower-heads so that they do not touch one another.

Range of air-drying material

Bunches of statice, roses, achillea and onions hang dry behind a vase of gypsophila standing in a little water. Cones and moss dry alongside artichoke heads supported by chicken wire.

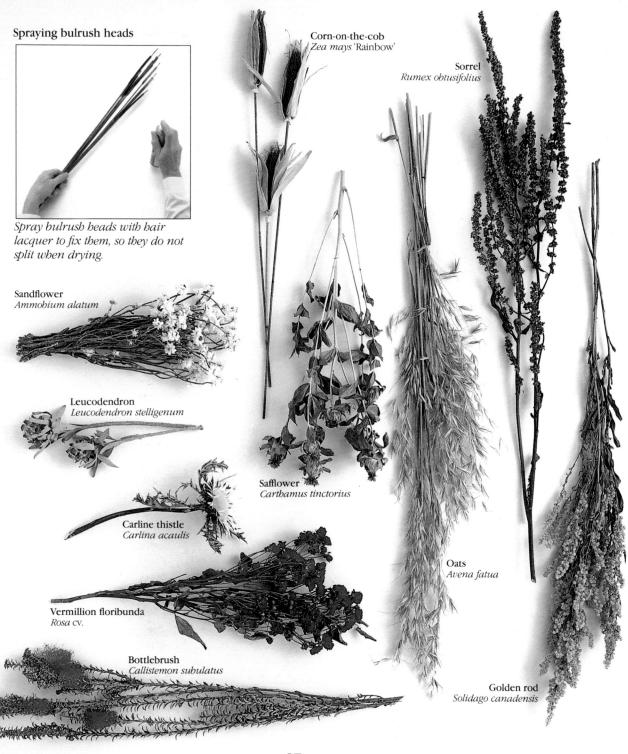

Spraying bulrush heads

Spray bulrush heads with hair lacquer to fix them, so they do not split when drying.

Corn-on-the-cob
Zea mays 'Rainbow'

Sorrel
Rumex obtusifolius

Sandflower
Ammobium alatum

Leucodendron
Leucodendron stelligenum

Carline thistle
Carlina acaulis

Safflower
Carthamus tinctorius

Vermillion floribunda
Rosa cv.

Bottlebrush
Callistemon subulatus

Oats
Avena fatua

Golden rod
Solidago canadensis

Pressing

One of the simplest ways of drying flowers and leaves is to press them. You can use a flower press, which you can either make yourself or buy, ready made, from a store. Alternatively, you can press small pieces of plant material between the pages of a heavy book, or, particularly for larger pieces of foliage, you can press material by placing it under a rug or carpet. Whichever method you use, you should always sandwich the plant material between sheets of absorbent paper, such as blotting paper, or newspaper. In this way, the plant material is both pressed and dried at the same time. If you are using a book, it is a good idea to pile other books on top for extra pressure.

Making and filling a press
There are several ways of making your own press. The simplest is to cut two pieces of plywood into identical rectangles about the same size as the covers of a large book. Bore four holes in each piece of wood, one at each corner. Insert a bolt into each hole in one piece of wood. The bolts should have wing-nuts, as they will be used to clamp the two pieces of wood together. Now cut out several rectangular pieces of blotting paper to fit within the area of the bolts and half that number of pieces of cardboard. Sandwich some plant material between two sheets of blotting paper, or a folded piece of blotting paper twice the size, and place on the bottom of the press. Cover with a sheet of cardboard, then add another plant material sandwich. Continue in this way – blotting paper, plant material, blotting paper, cardboard – until the press is full. The cardboard is important, as it prevents the impression of the plant ma-

terial passing through one layer of blotting paper to the next. Finish the giant sandwich with the second piece of wood, allowing the bolts in the first to pass through the holes in the second. Secure tightly with the wing-nuts.

You can make a larger press, similar to the one shown opposite, out of two pieces of hardwood. Instead of drilling holes in the corners for bolts to pass through, pull the two pieces of wood tightly together with nylon cord, binding them around cleats fixed to the top of the press.

Ideal plants for pressing
Some of the best flowers for pressing in a press or book are violas, pansies, primroses and hydrangeas (both mop-head and lace-cap), single roses, sweet peas, all daisy-like flowers, hellebores and poppies. Very full petalled, three-dimensional flowers do not press very well as it is difficult to arrange them flat, so that the overlapping petals will not become bent or lumpy as they are pressed. However, by choosing the growing flowers carefully and setting them, before pressing, on to an absorbent surface with their petals pointing in the right directions, even a double peony can emerge from the press looking beautiful. Small pieces of foliage, such as fern, *Senecio greyi*, choisya, stachys and single leaves from trees, are also ideal for placing in a press.

Larger pieces of foliage, such as beech, maple, ash, plane and bamboo, are best dried under a rug, carpet or mattress. Avoid placing them in a busy part of the house, where they are likely to be trampled over a lot and sandwich the plant material between thick layers of newspaper.

Lace-cap hydrangea
Hydrangea macrophylla

Pansy
Viola x *wittrockiana*

Senecio
Senecio greyi

Lamb's tongue *Stachys lan*

Using a press
You will need a press, blotting paper, cardboard and material for pressing. Place a piece of cardboard then a folded sheet of blotting paper on the base of the press. Insert the plant material in the blotting paper. Cover with another piece of cardboard. Continue until the press is full.

Pressing flowers with bulky centers
You will need a press, blotting paper, cardboard, styrafoam, a knife, scissors, plant material.
1 *Place the flowers on the bottom of the blotting paper and cut holes in the top to align with the flower centers. Fold over.*

2 *Cut a slice of foam to the same thickness as the flowers. Cut holes in it to align with the flower centers and place on top of the blotting paper. Place a piece of cardboard on top of the foam and continue loading the press, layering the material.*

Using a book
You can press material between blotting paper or newspaper in a book. Weight with other books.

Rough chervil
Chaerophyllum temulentum

Heron's bill
Erodium cicutarium

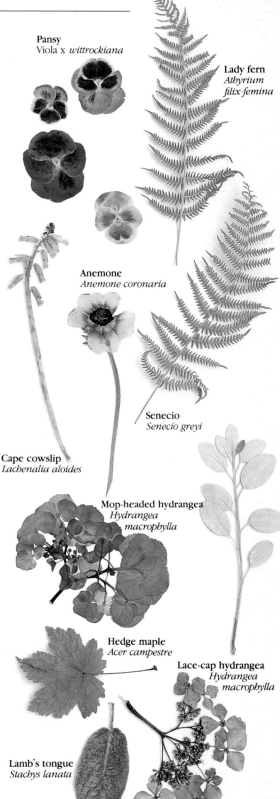

Pansy
Viola x wittrockiana

Lady fern
Athyrium filix-femina

Anemone
Anemone coronaria

Senecio
Senecio greyi

Cape cowslip
Lachenalia aloides

Mop-headed hydrangea
Hydrangea macrophylla

Hedge maple
Acer campestre

Lace-cap hydrangea
Hydrangea macrophylla

Lamb's tongue
Stachys lanata

Using Desiccants

Most plant material can be dried effectively using desiccants, or drying agents, such as silica gel, borax, alum or fine sand. Excellent results can be achieved with lilies, peonies, roses, freesias, narcissus, camellias and orchids. Desiccants draw the moisture out of the plant material while holding it firmly in place, so material dried by this method most closely resembles its fresh counterpart in color, size and texture. However, there are drawbacks to using desiccants. Silica gel, which dries material the quickest, is very expensive, and all desiccants are fiddly to place around the flowers that you are drying.

Moisture-free crystals

Before using a desiccant you must ensure that it is absolutely moisture-free. Silica gel crystals can be purchased with a color indicator built in. When the crystals are pink, they contain water; when they are deep blue they are completely dry. The crystals are quite large when you buy them and need to be ground down, roughly to the consistency of fine coffee. Do this in a coffee grinder or food processor, making sure that you clean the grinder thoroughly before using it for food again. The best way to dry the desiccant is to place it on a baking tray in the oven at a moderate temperature for an hour or so. Turn the oven off and allow the desiccant to cool inside, so that it is still moisture-free when you come to use it. If you don't want to use it immediately, store it in an air-tight container until you are ready to start the drying process. Borax and alum powders are best mixed with fine silver sand. You can use silver sand alone, although material takes longer to dry.

Freesia
Freesia x *kewensis*

Preparing the flowers

Flowers dried with desiccants need to be in absolutely prime condition. If you are picking them from your garden, make sure that they are as dry as possible by cutting them on a dry day in the afternoon.

Plant material dried in this way tends to become rather brittle, so it is often a good idea to wire the flower-heads before drying them. Avoid drying flowers with heavy stems by this method: the stem will not dry as quickly as the flower-head and either the flower will be too dry or the stem will be too moist and will rot once the plant is removed from the desiccant.

The drying process

You will need an air-tight box or tin large enough to hold the material you wish to dry. Firstly, place a layer of desiccant on the bottom of the container. Next, place the bloom on this layer and gradually pile the desiccant around the flower, using a fine brush to make sure that every part of each flower is surrounded by desiccant. Once the flowers are completely immersed, replace the lid of the container and seal it with sticky tape.

If you are using silica gel crystals then you should test for dryness after forty-eight hours. The crystals should have turned pink, depending on how much material you have dried. Take out the flowers very gently once you are sure that they are completely dry. Do not leave them in too long or they will become very brittle. Plant material dried in borax or alum powder mixed with silver sand will take about ten days to dry, and plant material placed in silver sand alone will take up to three weeks.

USING DESICCANTS

Using silica gel

You will need silica gel crystals, biscuit tin, spoon, paintbrush and flower-heads.
1 *Cover the base of the tin with crystals and place the flower-heads on top.*

2 *Spoon silica gel crystals around the flower-heads and ease the crystals between and on top of the petals with a brush. Replace the lid and seal. Leave for 48 hours.*

Peony
Paeonia lactiflora

Peruvian lily
Alstroemeria ligtu hybrid

Belladonna lily
Amaryllis belladonna

Persian buttercup
Ranunculus asiaticus

White rose
Rosa 'Gruss an Aachen'

Tulip
Tulipa 'Eros'

Peony
Paeonia lactiflora

Golden rose
Rosa 'Golden Times'

Parrot tulip
Tulipa sp.

Persian buttercup
Ranunculus asiaticus

Daffodil
Narcissus 'Golden Harvest'

Lily
Lilium 'Aristocrat'

Daffodil
Narcissus 'Sarah'

Lace-cap hydrangea
Hydrangea macrophylla 'Altona'

Lily
Lilium speciosum rubrum

Daffodil
Narcissus 'Cheerfulness'

101

Using Glycerine

Preserving plant material with glycerine does not depend on removing the moisture content from the plant, but rather on replacing the plant's water with glycerine, which keeps the plant in a stable condition over a long period. A small number of flowers can be preserved in this way, but for the most part it is leaves which are best suited to preservation with glycerine.

Preserving strong-stemmed material

For strong-stemmed material, make up a solution of sixty per cent almost boiling water to forty per cent glycerine and stir the mixture thoroughly. Cut the stems at a very sharp angle, and, if you are preserving brown, hardwood stems, hammer the ends as well. Place the plant material in a vase containing approximately 10cm (4in) of the hot solution, so that the stems are firmly supported by the sides of the container. Insert wire in hollow-stemmed material such as bells of Ireland to prevent them from keeling over. Place the vase in a cool, dark place and allow at least six days for absorption to take place. The process might well take about ten days to complete. When little beads of glycerine start to form on the upper part of the plant material the material has absorbed as much as it needs. Remove it from the solution immediately – plant material becomes soggy and limp if it over-absorbs glycerine – then wash the material thoroughly.

Preserving leaves

Most leaves of both deciduous and evergreen plants and trees can be preserved in glycerine, and it is a particularly good method for beech, copper beech, eucalyptus, ivy, mahonia and choisya leaves as well as moluccella, or bells of Ireland. Leaves are best picked at the height of summer when they are at their strongest and most mature. In fact, glycerine does not preserve immature plant material, so new spring leaves cannot be treated in this way.

Single leaves can be preserved by immersing them in a slightly stronger (fifty per cent glycerine, fifty per cent water) solution. Magnolia, holly, aspidistra, laurel, box, fatsia, elaeagnus, pittosporum and some silver-leaved plants, such as *Senecio greyi* and *Phlomis fruticosa*, can all be preserved in this way. Leaves immersed in glycerine take only about six days to absorb the solution. At this point you will notice a color change. Remove the leaves from the solution and wash them thoroughly in a water and washing-up liquid solution, before rinsing them in tap water. Finally, pat the leaves dry with absorbent kitchen paper.

Coloring preserved material

Glycerined plant material is as supple as if it were still growing. However, it also takes away much of the color and often tints leaves a muddy, dark shade.

To prevent material turning a murky color, simply add some water-soluble dye to the glycerine solution. This applies equally to leaves immersed in the solution and stems standing in the solution. Coppery red dye is particularly beneficial when preserving copper beech to help it retain its glowing, natural color. It will also give eucalyptus leaves an interesting, though natural-looking, color. Green dye is a good idea for most green leaves. For more ideas on coloring dried or drying material see p.106.

Clubmoss
Selaginella kraussiana

Lime
Tilia x *euchlora*

USING GLYCERINE

Preserving long-stemmed material

You will need *a vase, glycerine solution, scissors and plant material.*
1 *Remove leaves from the stem ends.*

2 *Cut stems at a sharp angle and place in a vase half filled with glycerine solution. Leave in a dark, cool place for ten days.*

Preserving foliage

You will need *a bowl, glycerine solution, soapy water and foliage.*
1 *Place foliage in glycerine solution.*

2 *Set the bowl in a dark place and leave until the leaves have darkened. Remove and wash in soapy water. Pat dry.*

Cider gum
Eucalyptus gunnii

Broad-leaved eucalyptus
Eucalyptus dalrympleana

Male fern
Dryopteris filix-mas

Lace-cap hydrangea
Hydrangea macrophylla

Bells of Ireland
Moluccella laevis

Copper beech
Fagus sylvatica 'Cuprea'

Crystallizing

Many flowers can be preserved by crystallizing them, a method which captures their natural, fresh beauty and makes them good to eat! Use crystallized flowers to decorate not only cakes, tarts and other puddings, but some savory dishes, too.

If you are planning to decorate food with crystallized flowers make sure that the plants you choose are not poisonous. In addition, when choosing flowers, make sure they are of a scale to suit the dish. It is a common mistake to use flowers that are too large for the surface of the cake.

Gum arabic or egg white?

There are two methods of crystallizing: in one you use gum arabic to preserve the plant material and in the other you use egg white. Flowers and leaves crystallized using gum arabic last for a long time. You can buy chocolates decorated with violets or rose petals, which have been crystallized by this method.

If you wish the plant material to last for many months you should use gum arabic. Dissolve 12g ($\frac{1}{2}$oz) gum arabic in $\frac{1}{4}$ cup of cold water in a double boiler or in a basin placed in a pan of simmering water. Stir until dissolved, then remove from the heat and allow the solution to cool. While it is cooling, make a syrup with $\frac{1}{4}$ cup of water and 100g (4oz) sugar. Boil to 80°C (230°F), then remove from the heat and allow to cool.

Apply the gum arabic solution to both sides of the leaves or petals of the flowers with a paintbrush. Next, brush on the sugar solution. Finally, sift fine sugar over the plant material until it is completely coated. Allow to dry on greaseproof paper.

Flowers crystallized using egg white look more beautiful than those crystallized using gum arabic, but they will not last for more than a few days and should be eaten within four or five days. However, as the life of a cake or tart is fairly short, this should not present a problem. To crystallize using egg white, beat the white of an egg until it is frothy and of an even consistency. Brush it on to the leaves or petals of the flowers, making sure that you give an even coating to both sides. Dredge fine sugar over the plant material so that it adheres and place the plant material on greaseproof paper. Place on a rack and leave in a warm place, such as an airing cupboard, above a radiator or in a very cool oven. The egg white will set and dry within a couple of hours.

The fragrant taste of flowers and leaves

Scented flowers will retain much of their perfume when they are crystallized, making them delicious to eat. Cherry, apple and pear blossoms are all fragrant-tasting, and so are acacia and elderflowers. Scented roses, violets, primroses and pansies all taste good when crystallized, while citrus blossom is a must. The taste of the petals of many flowers that grow from bulbs is not pleasant, although little scented narcissus are perfectly good to eat.

Crystallized leaves can look very attractive, especially when used to make a border on top of a cake. A rich chocolate cake with fresh mint icing and filling is made all the more luscious by the addition of a border of crystallized mint leaves. Lemon balm leaves and scented geranium leaves are excellent for this purpose, too. Slices of the stalk of *Angelica archangelica* are delicious when crystallized.

Primrose
Primula vulgaris

Lungwort
Pulmonaria saccharata

Almond blossom
Prunus dulcis 'Rosea-plena'

Daffodil
Narcissus Peeping Tom

CRYSTALLIZING

Crystallizing using egg white

You will need *lightly beaten egg white, finely granulated sugar, teaspoon, paintbrush, drying rack and flower-heads.*
1 *With a paintbrush cover the petals of a flower with egg white.*

2 *Holding the flower-head by the stem, dredge the fine sugar over the petals with a teaspoon. Make sure you cover the flower-head completely but shake off any surplus sugar.*

3 *Place on a rack to dry. The material will crystallize within a few hours if you place the rack in an airing cupboard. Decorate the top of a gâteau or tart and eat within four days.*

Almond blossom
Prunus dulcis 'Rosea-plena'

Pansy
Viola x *wittrockiana*

Almond blossom
Prunus dulcis 'Rosea-plena'

Pansy
Viola x *wittrockiana*

Chrysanthemum
Chyrsanthemum 'Penny Lane'

Primrose
Primula vulgaris

Squill
Scilla sibirica 'Spring Beauty'

Polyanthus primrose
Primula polyantha

Common camellia
Camellia japonica
'Adolphe Andersson'

mond blossom
Prunus dulcis
Rosea-plena'

Rose petal
Rosa cv.

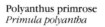

Daffodil
Narcissus 'Peeping Tom'

Polyanthus primrose
Primula polyantha

Primrose
Primula vulgaris

Coloring

Many festive arrangements benefit from the inclusion of some brightly colored dried-plant material, and you can enliven much tired-looking material enormously by coloring it. There are several methods of coloring plant material, which are carried out at different stages of the drying or preserving process.

Dyeing material preserved in glycerine

If you add dye to the glycerine solution the plant material will drink the dye at the same time as the solution. Leaf material often turns a rather muddy color while it is absorbing glycerine and adding some dye to the solution will help reduce its drab appearance. I recommend using a strong green dye for most green leaves. This will result in leaves that are darker than fresh leaves, but that will certainly look much more attractive than undyed material. The following foliage is ideal for dyeing in this way: beech, oak, maple, ivy, rhododendron, choisya, chestnut, ferns and even moss.

You can equally well dye foliage or flowers preserved in glycerine an artificial color. Try adding deep red dye to eucalyptus leaves to give them an authentic autumnal glow, and some rust-colored dye to lime bracts and copper beech leaves to give them a warm, mellow appeal.

Alternatively, you can add bleach to the glycerine solution. This acts in the same way as preserving the material in bright sunlight, removing most of the natural color and leaving the plant material a creamy color. Pale-colored hydrangea flower-heads and moluccella stems benefit from bleaching in this way as they have a tendency to turn paler during the glycerining process in any case.

Dyeing material as it air dries

If you are standing material in water before letting it air dry, you could add some dye to the water. The material will then drink the dye with the water before it starts to dry. It is important that the plant material should look absolutely natural when dried, so try to dye the material a color that actually exists in a variety of the plant that you are dyeing. *Erica arborea*, sea lavender and hydrangeas can be enhanced in this way. In general, blue is the least satisfactory color for dyeing, often producing extremely unnatural-looking plants.

Color spraying and painting

Special spray paints for coloring both fresh and dried flowers are available in a huge range of colors. Some are particularly useful. Sea lavender, which dries to a gray-white, can be sprayed a natural-looking pale yellow or pink. A combination of the two will result in an extremely attractive apricot or peach color.

Brighter color sprays or fast-drying paint are ideal for festive decorations where you want to create a splash of color. Poppy seed-heads and love-in-a-mist seed-heads look wonderful colored bright red, bright pink or rich green. All cones, nuts and the delicate umbels of lovage, cow parsley, coriander and fennel look great sprayed silver or gold and then dredged with glitter before the paint has dried, so that the sparkling crystals adhere well. However, for all-year-round arrangements it is best to use only colors that are less striking and more natural-looking, so that even when such an arrangement is closely examined there will seem to be absolutely nothing false about it.

Silver lichen
Cladonia sp.
dyed rich green

Spray painting

Taking three or four stems at once, spray poppy seed-heads thoroughly with red paint.

Glittering

Spray pine cones with silver paint. Then sprinkle glitter over them for extra sparkle.

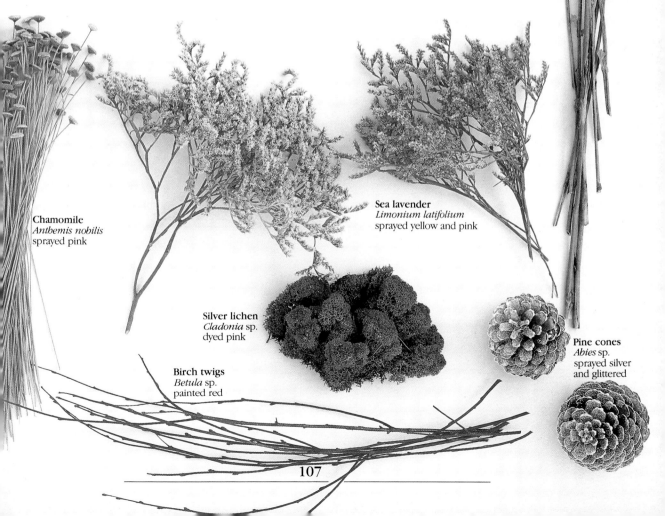

Poppy seed-heads
Papaver rhoeas
sprayed red

Chamomile
Anthemis nobilis
sprayed pink

Sea lavender
Limonium latifolium
sprayed yellow and pink

Silver lichen
Cladonia sp.
dyed pink

Birch twigs
Betula sp.
painted red

Pine cones
Abies sp.
sprayed silver
and glittered

Storing

If you are harvesting and drying or pressing your own material you will probably have periods of surplus, when you cannot possibly use all your recently dried material in arrangements. You may then need to store it for many months, in which case you will have to be careful about how and where you pack it.

Storing material where it dries

Any flowers that are hanging in bunches from the ceiling to dry can simply be left hanging after they have dried. However, storing material in this way is only a good idea if the bunches are out of direct sunlight. If the bunches are hanging in a very light position the colors of the flowers will soon fade. Equally, any material that you are drying in a cupboard, perhaps some large-headed flowers supported by chicken wire or some moss or cones in an open-topped box, can simply be left where they are until you are ready to use them.

Storing material in boxes

The usual method of storing material is to pack it away in sealed cardboard boxes, which are then placed in a cool, dry place, preferably with some ventilation. Before packing dried material ensure that it is completely dry. If there is still some moisture in just one flower, rot will soon set in once the box is packed, destroying all the dried flowers in the box.

The cardboard boxes used for packing fresh flowers when taking them to market are probably the most suitable for storing dried material. The size of box that you need will depend on the type of dried material that you wish to pack. If you want to store small bunches of flowers, not more than 30cm (1ft) long, then the sort of box that anemones are packed in – about 60cm (2ft) long, 37cm (1ft 3in) wide and 15cm (6in) deep – is ideal. For longer material, such as delphiniums, dock or bamboo, you will need a much longer box. Usually, flower shops are more than happy to sell you some flower boxes.

Packing a box

Air-dried plant material needs to be held firmly in place in such a way that no appreciable amount of pressure is placed on flower-heads, leaves or seed-heads. Large, delicate flower-heads, such as delphiniums, peonies, proteas and material dried using desiccants, are best wrapped singly in tissue paper before packing, so that each is well protected from its neighbor. Material that has delicate flower-heads can be bunched together and layered into the box. Wrap fragile bunches in tissue paper first. Pack the bunches so that the stalks of one layer are separated from the material in the next layer with strips of pleated tissue or soft newspaper.

Glycerined material should be packed in the same way. However, on no account pack glycerined and air-dried material in the same box, as plant material that has been preserved with glycerine will still retain some moisture and will therefore spoil dried flowers and foliage immediately.

You can also store pressed material in much the same way. Place it in a box, layering it between sheets of blotting paper, newspaper or tissue paper. Very strong material, such as all cones, artichokes and corn-on-the-cob heads, require no special protection and are best laid in a box or basket and stored in a cool, dry place until required.

Bunches of fragile-petalled roses should be wrapped in tissue paper before packing in a box.

Packing bunches
Place tissue paper between the stalks of one layer and the flower-heads of the next.

Wrapping large flower-heads
Swathe a large flower-head, such as a protea, peony or hydrangea head, with a doubled and pleated sheet of tissue paper and tie it around the stem.

ARRANGEMENTS FROM YOUR GARDEN

Contrasting forms of leptospermum flowers, oats and poppy seed-heads with Silene pendula.

*T*here can be few things more creative and rewarding than designing a garden. If you are fortunate enough to be starting from scratch – a rare occurrence – you will have the opportunity to plan a garden that will fulfil your needs exactly. So you can plant your selection of plants in the theme of your choice to create beds and borders that will not only look good throughout the year, but will also provide you with plenty of flowers and foliage for fresh arrangements and for drying.

To achieve this you will need to create a strong structure, not only of the layout of the beds, paving and grass areas, but of the plants themselves. Form is of primary importance when planning a garden. If you get this right, when you look out of your kitchen or living-room window during mid-winter, there will still be some interesting views. The garden will be more muted, of course, possibly with just the outlines of branches and stems against some of the stronger rich, dark evergreens.

With a careful choice of plants you can create a garden that remains beautiful after you have cut flowers for drying. The key is to include in your planting scheme a large variety of plants that can be dried or preserved and always cut only a proportion of the flowers, so as not to denude a border unduly. The choice of plants to grow, both for decorative garden purposes and for picking, is huge. There are climbers like roses, vines and clematis. Then for the borders there is a host of leaves and flowers that can be preserved: roses (of course!), lavender, most silver foliage plants, poppy and love-in-a-mist seed-heads, which you can enjoy in flower in the garden first, great hybrid delphiniums or little buttercups, peonies or Queen Anne's lace – the list is enormous.

Red, Orange and Yellow Border

These warm, sunny colors combine happily and are well represented in flower and foliage. Many of the flowering plants in this color range enjoy a sunny position, although a few will do best in a semi-shaded place. Again, it is possible to create a border, or even a whole garden, on this color theme, that will look attractive throughout the summer and autumn and also provide a good quantity of material for drying. With careful positioning of structural and evergreen plants, a garden can look interesting even in the depths of winter.

Red, orange and yellow roses

There are many favorite roses in this color range and both red and yellow roses are imbued with a fine scent, which is present in the rose for many months after it is picked. Hybrid tea roses are the most suitable for air drying. Of the reds, 'Highlight', 'Ena Harkness', 'Ernest H. Morse', 'Megiddo' and 'Fragrant Cloud' are all scented and have a good, firm shape. With yellow flowers 'King's Ransom', 'Chinatown', 'Kim' and 'Courvoisier' provide a variety of bush heights in a border. In the gold and orange range 'Redgold', 'Irene Churruca', 'Sutter's Gold', 'Beauté', 'Golden Treasure' and 'Whisky Mac' are all lovely.

Golden-leaved shrubs and trees

Some golden-leaved evergreens are useful plants to incorporate in the structure of a mixed shrub and perennial border. *Elaeagnus pungens* 'Maculata' has boldly splashed green and gold leaves, which can be preserved with glycerine, although the startling color will then be lost. *Euonymus japonica* 'Aureopictus' and *Griselinia littoralis* also provide a sunny look to the garden throughout the year.

Many trees have good autumn coloring. Among the best are maples. *Acer japonicum* 'Aureum' has golden leaves throughout the summer, which turn to glorious bright red in autumn. Cut maple branches at the peak of their color and press them under a carpet.

Flowers, seed-heads and foliage

Bamboo dries well and, although the leaves of *Arundinaria murielae* and *A. nitida* are clear green when fresh, they dry to a beautiful gray-green. Callistemon foliage air dries to a good, fresh, yellowy green. The flowers, too, can be air dried with ease and, together with *Helichrysum bracteatum,* they form some of the brightest reds in the whole range of flowers suitable for drying. *Helichrysum angustifolium,* or curry plant, and *H. splendidum* have silvery foliage and bright yellow heads of flowers. These are beautiful when used singly in small arrangements, or as bunches in larger arrangements. *Phlomis fruticosa* also has silver foliage and yellow whorls of flowers; you can either air dry the leaves and flowers or wait until later in the year and dry the seed-heads.

All achilleas produce good drying material. They mostly have flat heads of yellow flowers, though *Achillea millefolium* 'Cerise Queen' has pink flower-heads. Yellow-flowered dahlias are particularly fresh-looking when dried and varieties with tight-knit pompon petals can either be air dried, hanging upside-down, or dried using desiccants. *Limonium sinuatum* produces bright clear yellow flowers and some orangey-apricot ones and is the easiest of flowers to dry. *Calendula officinalis* is more difficult to dry. Unless it is picked in bud, just as it is beginning to show color, it will fragment once dry. However, it is worth a try, and the plants will provide a long succession of flowers throughout the whole summer and autumn.

Golden rod flowers in the autumn and some of the newer forms are very beautiful. Another quick spreader, but nevertheless a very beautiful plant, is *Alchemilla mollis,* or lady's mantle, with its froth of golden flowers which appear in early summer.

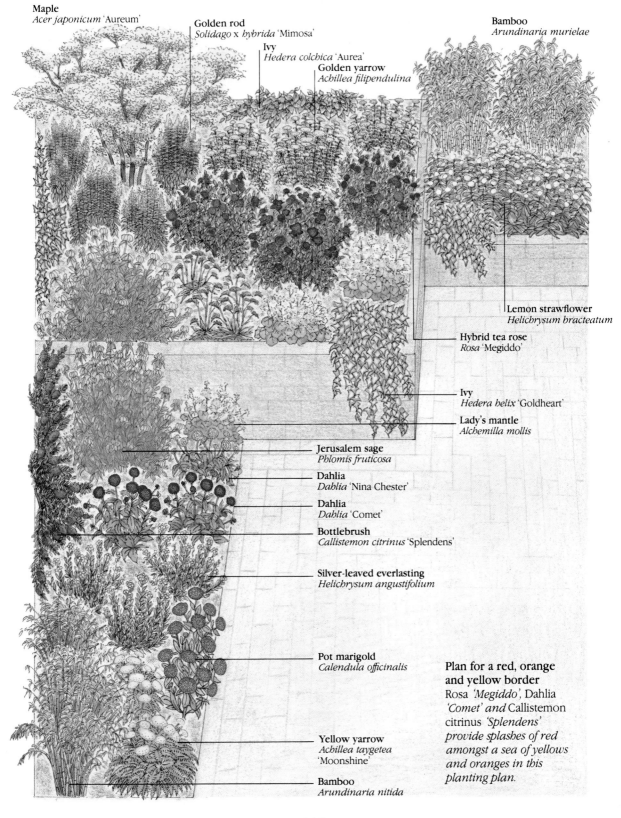

Maple
Acer japonicum 'Aureum'

Golden rod
Solidago x *hybrida* 'Mimosa'

Ivy
Hedera colchica 'Aurea'

Golden yarrow
Achillea filipendulina

Bamboo
Arundinaria murielae

Lemon strawflower
Helichrysum bracteatum

Hybrid tea rose
Rosa 'Megiddo'

Ivy
Hedera helix 'Goldheart'

Lady's mantle
Alchemilla mollis

Jerusalem sage
Phlomis fruticosa

Dahlia
Dahlia 'Nina Chester'

Dahlia
Dahlia 'Comet'

Bottlebrush
Callistemon citrinus 'Splendens'

Silver-leaved everlasting
Helichrysum angustifolium

Pot marigold
Calendula officinalis

Yellow yarrow
Achillea taygetea 'Moonshine'

Bamboo
Arundinaria nitida

Plan for a red, orange and yellow border
Rosa *'Megiddo',* Dahlia *'Comet' and* Callistemon citrinus *'Splendens' provide splashes of red amongst a sea of yellows and oranges in this planting plan.*

Red, orange and yellow dried flowers

All these flowers can be easily grown and dried. To achieve perfect-looking dahlia flowers it is best to dry them with a desiccant. Air dry the others by hanging them upside-down in bunches. The golden rod was picked just as it started to show color so that it could be used as a greeny filler.

Bottlebrush
Callistemon subulatus

Apricot statice
Limonium sinuatum

Curry plant
Helichrysum angustifolium

Pompon dahlia
Dahlia cv.

Strawflower or everlasting
Helichrysum bracteatum

Pompon dahlia
Dahlia cv.

Red rose
Rosa 'Nordia'

Golden rod
Solidago canadensis

Pompon dahlia
Dahlia cv.

Red, orange and yellow arrangement
This hot, sunny, wall-hanging arrangement in a broom twig basket is composed of orange helichrysum, callistemon, apricot-colored limonium, 'Megiddo' roses, red dahlias and golden Helichrysum angustifolium *with golden rod in the background.*

Pink, Blue and Silver Border

There are a huge number of plants that feature pink, blue, lilac or silver colors, dry easily and retain their color well. So you should have little difficulty creating a border that provides a good display of flower color and leaf form over a long period *and* supplies you with plenty of material for preserving. If you intersperse the plants in groups and pick only a proportion of the different kinds of flower at any one time for drying, the garden will not look sparsely planted.

Combining plants

When planning a garden or border it is important to consider how the plants will relate to one another; how the stems, leaves and flowers of each plant or group of plants will combine to form hills and valleys, spires, domes and arches. In this color range, pink roses associate particularly well with plants which have silver foliage, such as lavender, rosemary, *Senecio greyi*, santolina and stachys.

Although roses are not the most beautifully shaped shrubs, they are an absolute must in any garden. Choose roses that are well scented – there seems to be little point to a rose without scent – and for drying purposes, choose hybrid tea roses with a good, firm shape.

Sadly, neither the beautiful old roses that open fully quartered nor the single roses air dry very well, although they can be successfully dried with sand, borax or silica gel. Pick rose buds that are just about to open on a dry day, preferably in the late morning when humidity is at its lowest. Then hang them in small bunches in a cool, dark drying space, separating the heads and removing the lower leaves and thorns (see p.94).

Planning the border

If the border is situated in a good light position try interplanting a group of roses with lavender and misty, blue-gray eryngium. Plant delphiniums behind, and some double-flowered peonies next to them. These not only have wonderful flowers and a good scent, but beautiful foliage as well. Lavender and eryngium can both be air dried. Peony flowers can be air dried, but, like old roses, you will achieve better results by using chemicals. Their leaves also press well.

At the front of the bed, *Stachys lanata* or lamb's ear will provide an attractive foil for the taller plants. Its silver, woolly flower-heads air dry easily and they give interesting shapes and texture to arrangements. Groups of annuals such as larkspur, helipterum, nigella and papaver provide color over a long period in summer, and the nigella and papaver seed-heads are ready for drying as soon as they are well formed. It is a good idea to include some *Senecio greyi* – a large, low, mound-forming plant with silver leaves and nodding silver buds. The buds should be picked for drying well before the yellow flowers start to open.

More planting suggestions

Hydrangeas do really well in a shady border. Their color will depend on the type of soil and, although they prefer acid conditions, they will thrive in almost any type of soil. Try grouping them under the dappled shade of a tree – a eucalyptus (where hardy) is ideal for such a situation. Always buy a small plant, as this will make a strong root system soon after it is planted and will therefore be unlikely to blow down when it has grown tall.

If you have a boundary wall or fence, then cover it in climbers and wall shrubs. Roses, clematis, *Hydrangea petiolaris* and ivy can all be preserved. The climbing roses 'Handel' and 'New Dawn' fit in very well with this color range, and the wall shrub *Ceanothus* 'A. T. Johnson' has wonderful blue flowers. They are, however, difficult to dry, although you might like to try using desiccants.

Snow gum tree
Eucalyptus niphophila

Mop-headed hydrangea
Hydrangea macrophylla
'Generale Vicomtesse de Vibraye'

Plan for a pink, blue and silver border

Set groups of pink roses, peonies, helipterum, lamb's tail and larkspur amongst a wealth of blue flowers – lavender, roses, larkspur, hydrangea, cornflowers, ceanothus, sea holly and senecio – to create a lovely lilac-tinged border.

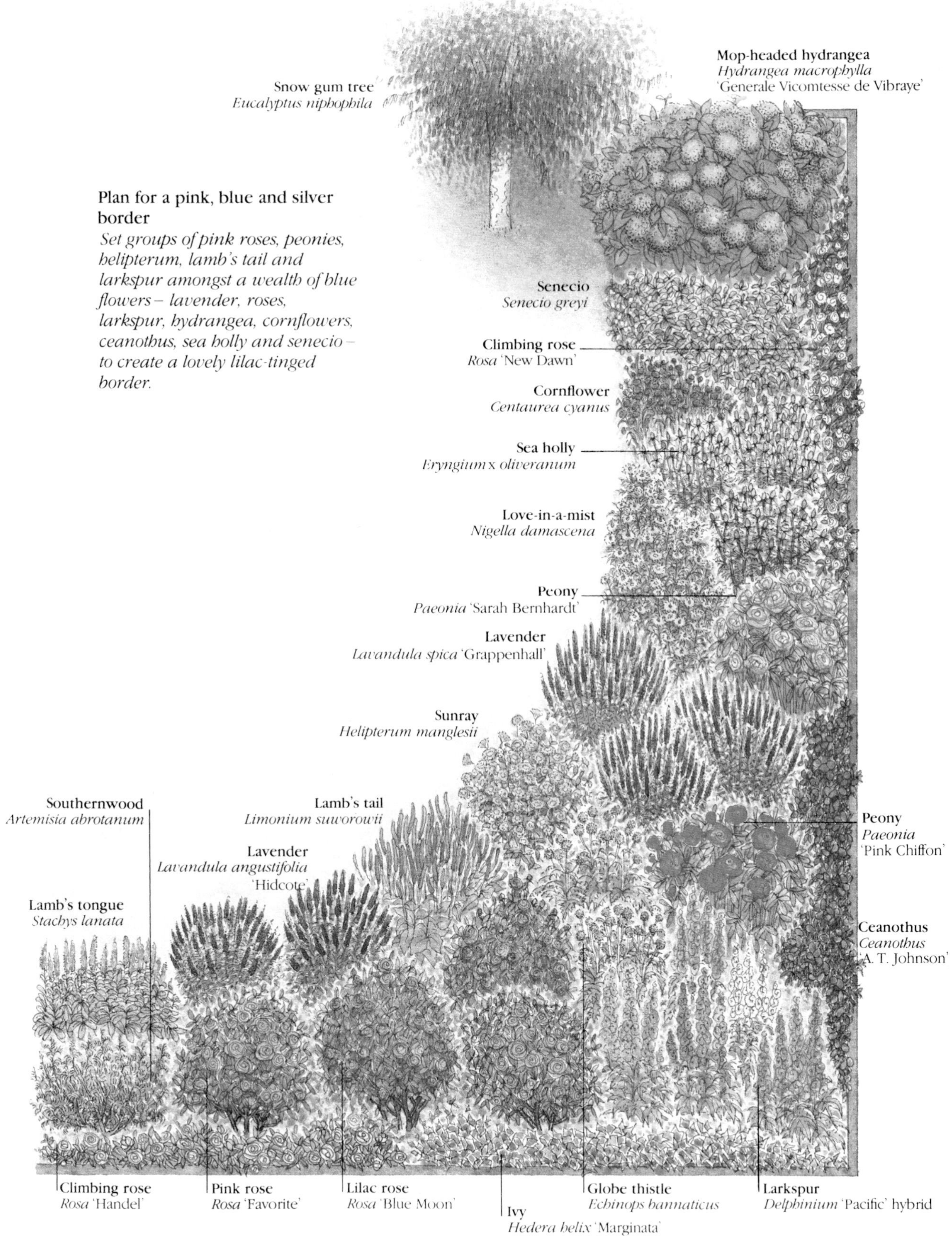

Senecio
Senecio greyi

Climbing rose
Rosa 'New Dawn'

Cornflower
Centaurea cyanus

Sea holly
Eryngium x *oliveranum*

Love-in-a-mist
Nigella damascena

Peony
Paeonia 'Sarah Bernhardt'

Lavender
Lavandula spica 'Grappenhall'

Sunray
Helipterum manglesii

Southernwood
Artemisia abrotanum

Lamb's tail
Limonium suworowii

Lavender
Lavandula angustifolia
'Hidcote'

Peony
Paeonia
'Pink Chiffon'

Lamb's tongue
Stachys lanata

Ceanothus
Ceanothus
'A. T. Johnson'

Climbing rose
Rosa 'Handel'

Pink rose
Rosa 'Favorite'

Lilac rose
Rosa 'Blue Moon'

Ivy
Hedera helix 'Marginata'

Globe thistle
Echinops bannaticus

Larkspur
Delphinium 'Pacific' hybrid

Pink, blue and silver dried flowers
All the dried plant material on these pages would look well in a pink, blue and silver border. Apart from the hydrangea, all the plants thrive in sunny positions and prefer a well-drained soil. The hydrangea prefers a cool, semi-shaded position and moist soil.

Senecio
Senecio greyi

Silver cypress
Kochia sp.

Globe thistle
Echinops ritro

Peony
Paeonia lactiflora

Mop-headed hydrangea
Hydrangea macrophylla 'Altona'

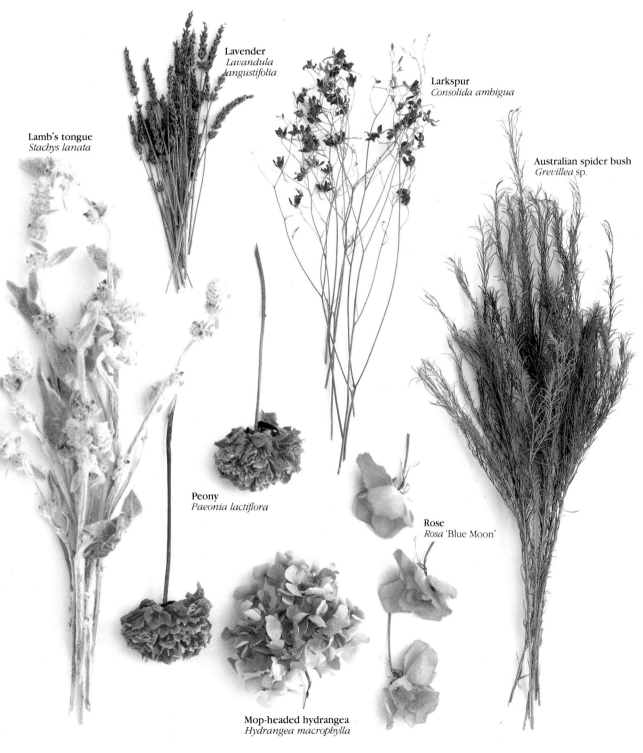

Lavender
*Lavandula
angustifolia*

Larkspur
Consolida ambigua

Lamb's tongue
Stachys lanata

Australian spider bush
Grevillea sp.

Peony
Paeonia lactiflora

Rose
Rosa 'Blue Moon'

Mop-headed hydrangea
Hydrangea macrophylla

Pink, blue and silver arrangement
The pink and lilac luster of this wonderful art nouveau vase provides the perfect foil for flowers and foliage in this color range. 'Blue Moon' roses, peonies and hydrangeas are set off by silver foliage, tufts of lavender and fine spikes of larkspur.

The Picking Garden

If you are fortunate enough to own a large garden, you might like to put aside an area in which you grow plants solely for drying. As this garden area will be designed chiefly to provide an abundance of flowers to pick for drying, you will probably prefer to situate it away from the decorative part of the garden and to set out the plants in formal rows like a vegetable garden to make flowers easy to harvest. Here, it is a good idea to grow some of the plants that do not look so good when grown in decorative beds, or which do not look very attractive once the flowers are harvested.

The majority of plants that can be preserved require a sunny, light position to grow well. Soil type is important, too. A strongly acid soil restricts the number of plants you can grow for preserving. However, if your soil is anything from mildly acid to moderately alkaline, you can grow an enormous number of plants with flowers, foliage and seed-heads that can be preserved for arranging.

Hybrid tea roses

The flowers of roses are immensely attractive, both fresh and dried, although the shrubs themselves often do not make a very good shape. So roses are a good choice for growing in the picking garden. Grow the varieties that will dry well and produce good crops of flowers in colors that will be suitable for your arrangements. There are plenty of roses to choose from. Firmly formed hybrid tea roses are easiest for air drying, so choose these for the picking garden and avoid single-flowered or old-fashioned varieties or roses that have lax petals, unless you are going to dry them with chemicals. Of the red hybrid teas, 'Red Devil', 'Megiddo' and 'Nordia' are all excellent. In the pink to peach range try 'Blessings', 'Wendy Cussons', 'Silva' and 'Chanelle'. Some good yellows are 'Golden Times', 'Golden Melody' and 'Courvoisier'.

Other plants to grow for drying

No picking garden should be without several varieties of achillea. Try to include the well-known, large-headed yellow *Achillea filipendulina*, *A. millefolium* 'Cerise Queen', with its pink flowers, *A. ptarmica* with its button-shaped white flowers and *A. taygetea* 'Moonshine' with its heads of pale yellow flowers.

Helichrysum and limonium feature in many of my dried-flower arrangements. You can grow them in a wide range of colours: *Helichrysum bracteatum*, the magnificent strawflower, is available in pinks, yellows, orange, red, cream and white. Daisy-flowered helipterums dry with great ease and come with pink, white and yellow flowers. *Gomphrena globosa* and *Alchemilla mollis* will also air dry very easily, and the alchemilla carries golden feathery flowers abundantly in early summer.

Celosia cristata has yellow, crimson and orange cockscomb-like flowers which you can use whole in large arrangements or split into sections to use in smaller ones. Both the flowers and the seed-heads of *Nigella damascena* can be dried, depending on when you harvest them. The plant has beautiful pale blue flowers in summer followed by large, green-striped rust seed-heads. The perennial *Gypsophila paniculata* will air dry simply by setting it in a vase in a small amount of water, which will gradually evaporate. It grows into a large, dome-shaped bush that is completely covered in flowers in summer. The variety 'Bristol Fairy' has tiny double white flowers and 'Pink Fairy', double pink flowers.

Some other plants you might like to choose for the picking garden are scabious, eryngium, globe thistle, amaranthus, ammobium, lunaria and Chinese lantern, as all of these produce excellent drying material. Many of the annuals are self-seeding and you can collect the seeds each year and resow them to produce the following year's plants.

Plan for a picking garden
Although it features only twelve types of plants, this picking garden looks attractive and provides plenty of material for drying.

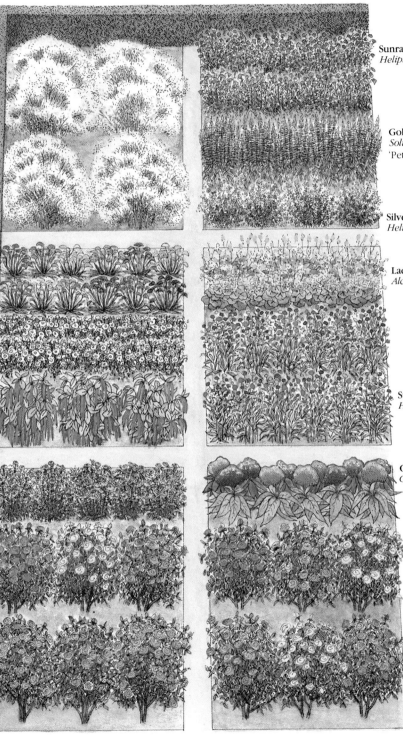

Sunray
Helipterum manglesii

Golden rod
Solidago canadensis
'Peter Pan'

Silver-leaved everlasting
Helichrysum angustifolium

Baby's breath
Gypsophila paniculata
'Bristol Fairy'

Statice
Limonium sinuatum
'New Art Shades'

Lady's mantle
Alchemilla mollis

Winged everlasting
Ammobium alatum

Strawflower
Helichrysum bracteatum

Prince's feather
Amaranthus caudatus

Love-in-a-mist
Nigella damascena

Cockscomb
Celosia cristata

Peach, pink, yellow
and lilac roses
Rosa cv.

Dried flowers from the picking garden

The scope for a wide variety of arrangements is large if you devote a section of your garden purely to growing flowers for drying. All these ingredients have been used in different combinations in the three jug arrangements on page 128.

Lady's mantle
Alchemilla mollis

Peach rose
Rosa 'Silva'

Strawflower
Helichrysum bracteatum

Cockscomb
Celosia cristata

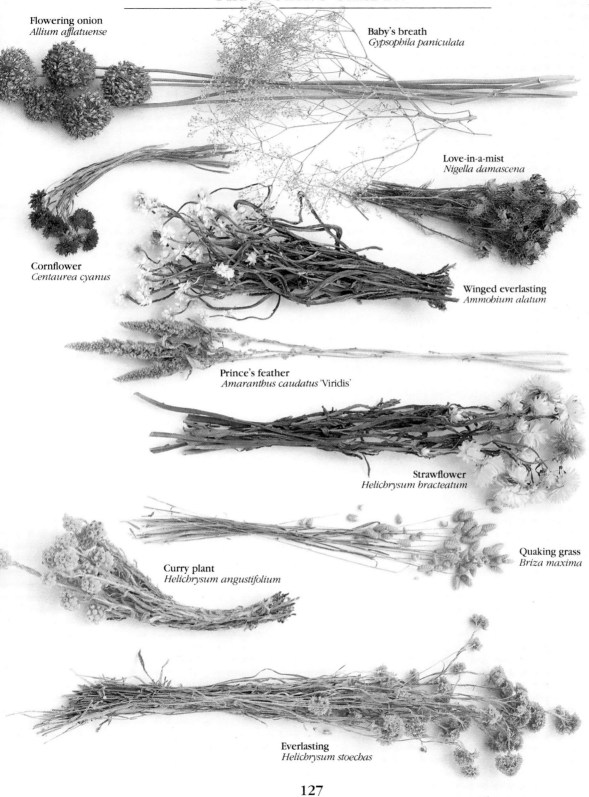

Flowering onion
Allium afflatuense

Baby's breath
Gypsophila paniculata

Love-in-a-mist
Nigella damascena

Cornflower
Centaurea cyanus

Winged everlasting
Ammobium alatum

Prince's feather
Amaranthus caudatus 'Viridis'

Strawflower
Helichrysum bracteatum

Curry plant
Helichrysum angustifolium

Quaking grass
Briza maxima

Everlasting
Helichrysum stoechas

Light and airy arrangement
The delicate pink and blue pattern on this tall, slim jug is picked up by gypsophila, love-in-a-mist and cornflowers. These fine-stemmed, delicate-looking flowers lend themselves well to a soft, airy arrangement.

Warm, summery arrangement
Alchemilla, rich red celosia heads, peach roses and deep pink helichrysum fill this gently curving jug (right).

Sunny arrangement
The flower design and pinky-gold luster of this fairly wide jug (below) are echoed by the shape and colors of the flowers.

Sunny and Shady Beds

Most annuals and biennials like the sunshine: they usually look good planted in small groups among a variety of shrubs and other perennial plants.

It is important to plant a strong structure of good-sized shrubs, including some evergreens, in a sunny bed so that it will look attractive not only during the flowering season, but throughout the whole year.

Plants that do best in shaded positions are mostly green foliage plants, and somehow this seems entirely right. The brighter colors, which do so well in sunny positions, would look out of place in a cooler, shady place, although small touches of bright color, such as the reds and pinks of annual impatience – plants that enjoy the shade – can make the denser green foliage seem all the more vibrant.

The sunny border

Most silver-foliage plants, such as anaphalis, artemisia, santolina, lavender, rosemary, senecio, sedum and salvia are sun lovers. Roses also need the sun and, if they are well-fed and watered during the summer months, the perpetual flowering varieties will continue to produce flowers from mid-summer until late autumn and there will even be the odd bud in early winter.

The planting plan for a sunny border (see p.131) features plants in the pink, silver, cream and lemon-yellow range. All the plants will yield material for preserving. Both types of rose featured are perpetual flowering: as usual, pick buds that are just starting to open for the drying rack. Heaths (*Erica* spp. and cvs.) and heather (*Calluna vulgaris* and cvs.) also need sun and a humusy, acid soil that is well drained. In neutral and slightly alkaline soils, incorporate large quantities of peat moss in the soil before planting. In mild climates, the tree heath (*Erica arborea*) will grow to 3m (10ft) or more. Pick heath and heather when in bud and spray the foliage with hair lacquer before hanging to dry.

Sedums take a long time to dry because of their fleshy stems. In fact, they will often produce fresh green shoots several weeks after they have been hung up to dry. Gypsophila is easy to dry. Simply cut the stems and then place them in a vase containing a little water and a drop or two of bleach. The liquid will evaporate away, leaving the gypsophila perfectly dried. *Moluccella laevis*, or bells of Ireland, preserves well in glycerine (see p.102). Remember to pick flowers for air drying about four days before they reach perfection. Also try to pick them in dry weather, and after any dew has evaporated.

The shady border

Planted in the shade of trees or perhaps a wall, ferns, hellebores and hostas come into their own. Fern fronds are incredibly beautiful and there are so many neglected varieties. Some, like cyrtomium, polystichum and phyllitis, are evergreen. All of them are easy to press and, because they are fairly two-dimensional when growing, pressed fronds look wonderfully natural when used in arrangements (see p.7). Both the leaves and flowers of hellebores can be pressed and, of course, the flowers can also be dried using a desiccant. The extremely decorative leaves of hostas can also be pressed and, after flowering, the seeding flower stems can be cut and dried. The flowers of hydrangea, which tolerates some shade, can be air dried.

Many evergreen shrubs and trees like a shaded or semi-shaded position: aucuba, azalea, box, camellia, elaeagnus, euonymus, fatsia, griselinia, holly, mahonia, privet and rhododendron all produce attractive flowers too. All these flowers can be dried using desiccants. Ivies and evergreen honeysuckle make perfect climbers for walls and fences and there are a host of other plants that can look very beautiful in combination throughout the year, supplying you with plenty of material for drying and preserving.

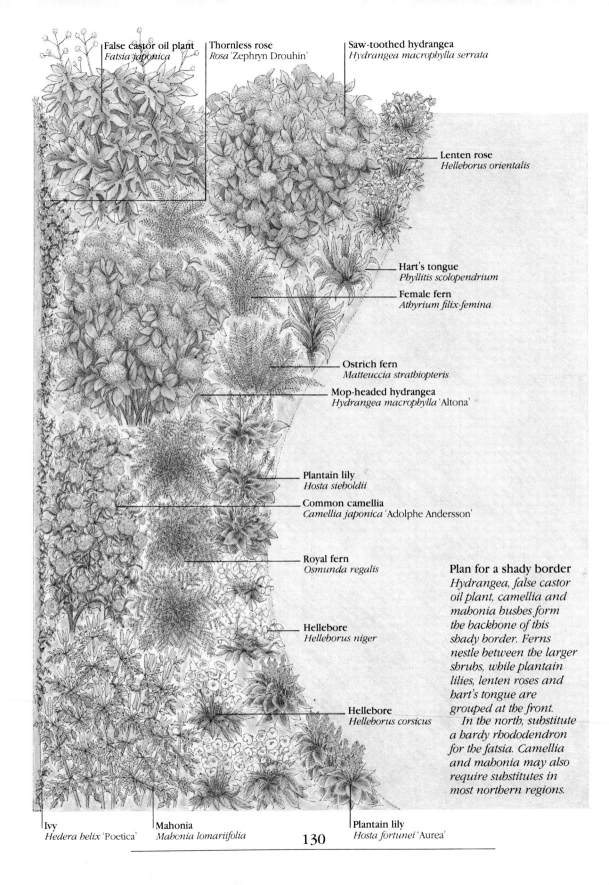

False castor oil plant
Fatsia japonica

Thornless rose
Rosa 'Zephryn Drouhin'

Saw-toothed hydrangea
Hydrangea macrophylla serrata

Lenten rose
Helleborus orientalis

Hart's tongue
Phyllitis scolopendrium

Female fern
Athyrium filix-femina

Ostrich fern
Matteuccia strathiopteris

Mop-headed hydrangea
Hydrangea macrophylla 'Altona'

Plantain lily
Hosta sieboldii

Common camellia
Camellia japonica 'Adolphe Andersson'

Royal fern
Osmunda regalis

Hellebore
Helleborus niger

Hellebore
Helleborus corsicus

Plan for a shady border
Hydrangea, false castor oil plant, camellia and mahonia bushes form the backbone of this shady border. Ferns nestle between the larger shrubs, while plantain lilies, lenten roses and hart's tongue are grouped at the front.
In the north, substitute a hardy rhododendron for the fatsia. Camellia and mahonia may also require substitutes in most northern regions.

Ivy
Hedera helix 'Poetica'

Mahonia
Mahonia lomariifolia

130

Plantain lily
Hosta fortunei 'Aurea'

Smoke tree
Cotinus coggygria 'Purpureus'

Lavender cotton
Santolina neapolitana

Cream rose
Rosa 'Chanelle'

Pearly everlasting
Anaphalis margaritacea

Baby's breath
Gypsophila paniculata

Spectacular sedum
Sedum spectabile 'Autumn Joy'

Bells of Ireland
Moluccella laevis

Golden rod
Solidago canadensis 'Lemore'

Lemon rose
Rosa 'Northern Lights'

Sage
Salvia splendens 'Salmon'

Tree heath
Erica arborea

Plan for a sunny border
*Featuring
predominantly pink and
light yellow flowers, this
sunny border has a
wistful, summery feel to
it. Baby's breath, tree
heath and lavender
cotton add unusual
textures.*

Wild-flower Border

The wild-flower border or garden requires a lot of work to keep it looking wild, while allowing each group of plants to grow unimpeded by the more rampant members of the community, but it is well worth the effort. Many garden plants are cultivars taken from wild plants, and some of them retain the informal, natural look of flowers of the countryside.

Shady and sunny sites

Shady beds tend to have a wild look. Use groups of violas and pansies, primroses and hellebores toward the front of a border and ferns and foxgloves behind them. In woodland areas, these introduced plants blend with native wild-flowers and ferns.

For sunnier positions, there are a wealth of wild plants and closely related garden plants to choose from. None of the following would look out of place in either a meadow or wild garden: grasses, euphorbias, lilies, veronicas, forget-me-nots, mulleins, limonium, campanulas, scabious, viburnums, roses, thistles, golden rod, California poppy, Sumac, annual larkspur, black-eyed Susan, Queen, and dock.

A natural-looking planting

The wild-flower garden plan on page 133 is for a section of land situated beside a slow-moving stream. It is part of a large garden and would need to be cultivated as a wild-flower border, for the giant hogweed would soon take over if its seedlings were not removed each year. Allow only one or maybe two plants to produce their astounding trunk-like stems with rays of white flowers followed by geometric seed formation.

At the other end of the scale, the primroses, violets and narcissus can all be pressed or preserved with desiccants. Additionally, the primulas, violet and primrose flowers are delicious to eat, once crystallized (see p.104).

Caltha palustris, the marsh marigold, must be grown either in shallow water or just on the edge of the water for best results. You can air dry the flowers by hanging them up or you can dry them with desiccants. Bulrushes like to grow in water up to about 1m (3ft) deep. If you have less water space available, plant the dwarf bulrush, *Typha minima*, in its place.

Miscanthus, chenopodium and fennel can all be air dried simply by standing them in a vase. You can use dried stalks of fennel when barbecuing fish. Lay the stalks on to glowing charcoal: their aromatic smoke imparts a delicious flavor to the fish. The annual larkspur is best dried by hanging it upside-down, while cornflowers and scabious are better dried more quickly, hanging in a hot airing cupboard or even in a warm oven, so that they will retain more of their color.

Hellebores are beautiful plants. Their flowers have a subtle character and vary in color from the pinks and plums of *Helleborus orientalis* to the almost black of the 'Black strain' cultivar, and from the pure white of *Helleborus niger* to the rich green of *Helleborus viridis* and *Helleborus foetidus*. The flowers can be dried using desiccants or pressed between sheets of blotting paper under a pile of books or in a press.

In the sunniest part of this wild garden, poppies will flower then form their beautifully shaped seed-heads. In the shadiest spot, under the tree, the nodding heads of comfrey will soon spread their seed to surround the trunk.

Considering the overview

If you are thinking of planting a small area of the garden with wild flowers, then choose plants that will fit in with the surrounding planting. For instance, a group of wild *Iris foetidissima* would sit beautifully in a herbaceous border that already contained clumps of cultivated iris. However, the flowers of *Iris foetidissima* are rather insignificant. It is the glowing red seed-heads, which appear in autumn and can be air dried, that provide the color.

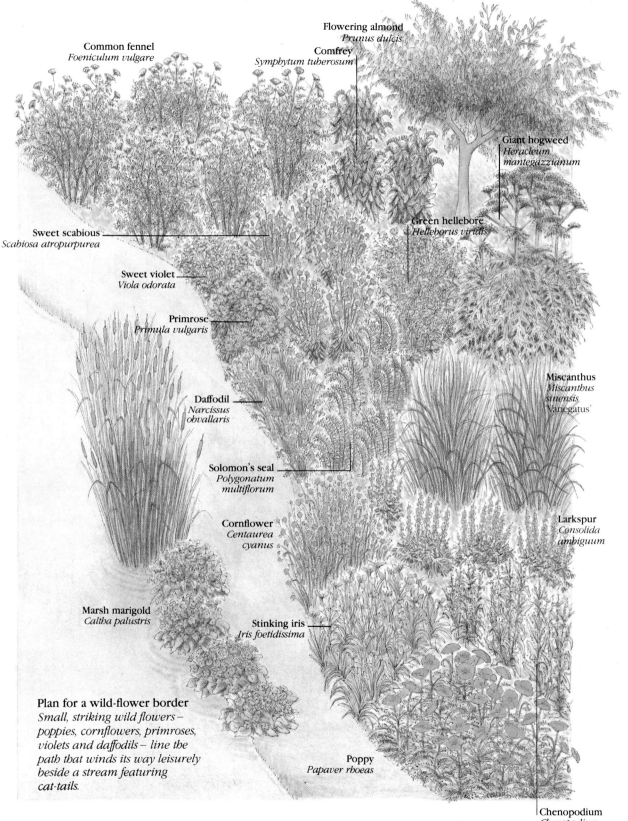

Flowering almond
Prunus dulcis

Comfrey
Symphytum tuberosum

Common fennel
Foeniculum vulgare

Giant hogweed
Heracleum mantegazzianum

Green hellebore
Helleborus viridis

Sweet scabious
Scabiosa atropurpurea

Sweet violet
Viola odorata

Primrose
Primula vulgaris

Miscanthus
Miscanthus sinensis
'Variegatus'

Daffodil
Narcissus obvallaris

Solomon's seal
Polygonatum multiflorum

Larkspur
Consolida ambiguum

Cornflower
Centaurea cyanus

Marsh marigold
Caltha palustris

Stinking iris
Iris foetidissima

Plan for a wild-flower border
Small, striking wild flowers –
poppies, cornflowers, primroses,
violets and daffodils – line the
path that winds its way leisurely
beside a stream featuring
cat-tails.

Poppy
Papaver rhoeas

Chenopodium
Chenopodium ficifolium

133

ADDITIONAL INFORMATION AND PLANT GUIDE

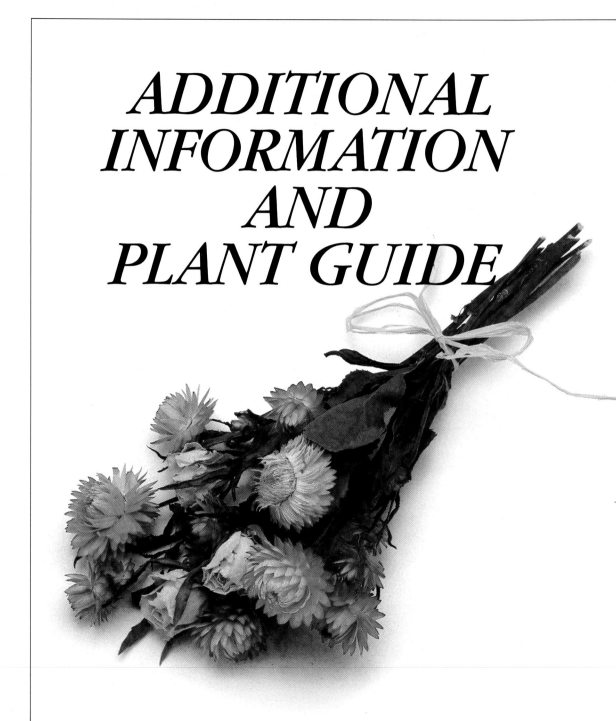

Rosa *'Gerda' nestle amongst* Helichrysum bracteatum *in this simple posy.*

*I*n this last section you will find some helpful tips on putting the finishing touches to your arrangements, from a simple bow for a posy to creating a loop for a hanging wreath. Bows often appear difficult to make, but you will find that with a little practice a simple ribbon bow will soon pose no problem.

Also included in this section is a résumé of all the essential tools and materials you will need for arranging dried flowers. Arranging flowers is basically a very simple process. Apart from the most important ingredients – the dried flowers and the container – there are only a few pieces of essential equipment to help you create a really professional-looking arrangement. A good pair of florists' scissors that will cut not only plant stems but ribbon and wire, too, is the most important piece of equipment. In addition, lengths of florist wire, styrafoam and chicken wire, are all essential for the keen arranger of dried flowers.

Finally, but perhaps most importantly, there is a plant guide to help you choose plant material for arranging. Whether you are gathering material from your garden to dry and use in arrangements or buying it from a shop, the plant guide will be a practical help. Covering the plant material used in the book, it outlines the conditions under which it grows best, advises when to harvest and the most suitable methods of drying or preserving it, describes the size of the material and suggests the most useful parts of the plant for arranging when dried. Lastly, it provides a quick reference to where the material is used in arrangements in the book, so that you can see the enormous range of possibilities when arranging your own selection of dried flowers.

Finishing Touches

Putting the finishing touches to an arrangement is just as important as arranging the flowers themselves. Without the concealing tie, the touch of ribbon, the flamboyant bow or the raffia loop, the bouquet, wreath, garland or even container arrangement will not look quite right: it will not be complete. The quality of the finishing touch will affect the quality of the whole arrangement so it is worth spending time perfecting a few finishing techniques.

Colorful ribbons
Particularly if you are giving a bouquet, it is the bow that makes the arrangement. Of course, you can go to a florist and buy a ready-made bow to affix to your arrangement, which will probably look perfect and just so, but it is much more rewarding to make your own, individual bow, and there are many different materials from which to choose.

Ribbons and tying tapes are available in a wide range of colors and materials ranging from satin and velvet ribbon, which comes in various widths and can be bought at a garden center or florist, to tear ribbon that is about 5cm (2in) wide when bought but which you can tear vertically into any narrower width. Tear ribbon looks like satin ribbon but is usually a little stiffer. It has one advantage over satin and other ribbons: it will twirl into curly ends if pulled tightly across the back edge of a knife or pair of scissors.

Making a bow
Making bows is much simpler than you might imagine. You simply make one or two figures-of-eight with the ribbon, overlapping each figure-of-eight. Pleat the center at the back where all the strips cross and tie the strips together firmly at this point with spool wire or a thin piece of ribbon or tying tape. If you use this wire then you will need to cover it with a piece of ribbon. You can usually use the same ribbon with which

you attach the bow to the arrangement. If you make the bow from tear ribbon or thin tying tape then you can divide the ends and make them twirl using the back of a knife.

Raffia, straw and twigs
Other, more natural, materials, such as raffia, straw and supple twigs, can be used to make a bow or finishing decoration. Raffia is my favorite and you can use it in its natural state or you can color it first. For a small arrangement, posy or bouquet, hold together a series of loops of raffia about 15cm (6in) in diameter and twist them into a figure-of-eight, so that you form two sets of loops each approximately 7.5cm (3in) in diameter. Make a raffia tie at the crossing point and use the ends of the tie to attach the bow to the arrangement. This can easily be pulled into a circlet of raffia loops.

Alternatively, you can plait strands of raffia and then make the whole plait into a bow. Plaited raffia also makes an attractive decorative loop for a larger, hanging arrangement, such as a wreath or garland.

Using florist wire
The simplest way to make a hanging device is to use florist wire. Loop the center of the wire to form a hanging ring and then thread the two ends through the wreath or hanging bunch and secure tightly. You can disguise any florist wire that is showing with a raffia or ribbon bow to suit the arrangement.

You can also use this wire like a needle to pull a length of ribbon through either the frame of a wreath or through the stalks of a bunch of flowers. The ribbon both secures the arrangement and forms a decorative bow, or attachment for a bow. Ribbon used in this way tends to collect dust and if it is used on a more permanent arrangement, such as a hanging bunch, it should be replaced as soon as it begins to look tired.

Making a straightforward bow

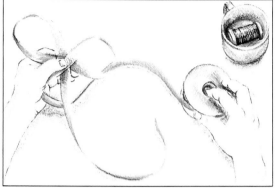

1 *Leave a length of ribbon to trail, then loop the ribbon into a figure-of-eight.*

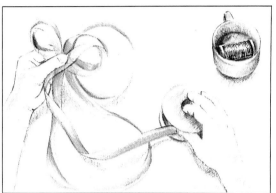

2 *Holding the center of the figure-of-eight, make a second figure-of-eight on top of the first.*

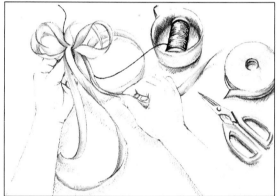

3 *Pleat the center of the loops in at the back and bind and knot with spool wire.*

4 *Bind the bunch with another piece of the same ribbon, covering the wire and leaving two loop ends.*

5 *Place the bow on top of the knot of the ribbon, bind the stems and pull out the ends of the binding ribbon.*

6 *Tie the bow in position with the ends of the binding ribbon. Cut the ends and tease into shape.*

Making a complicated bow

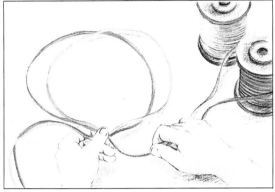

1 *Taking two narrow-width ribbons, loop them to-gether to create a circle about 25cm (10in) across.*

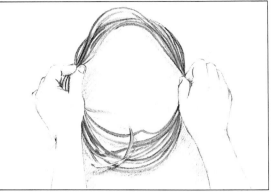

2 *Continue looping the ribbons until eight circles are piled on top of one another. Pull out the circles.*

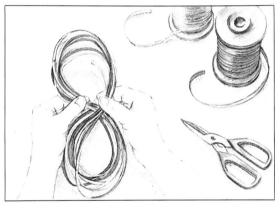

3 *Holding the ribbons at the widest point, make a figure-of-eight.*

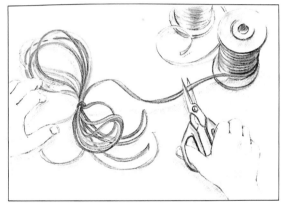

4 *Take another piece of matching narrow ribbon and tie the figure-of-eight securely at the center.*

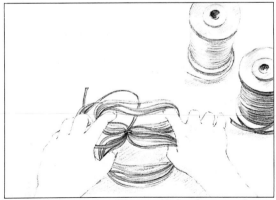

5 *Gently loosen the ribbons with forefinger and thumb to create a full-looking bow.*

6 *Tie the bow to the bouquet with the ribbon that is binding the bunch.*

Making a wire loop

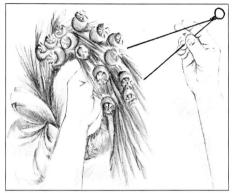

1 *Take a florist wire and cover with floral tape. Twist at the center.*

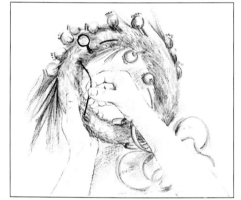

2 *Push the ends of the florist wire into and out of the back of the base.*

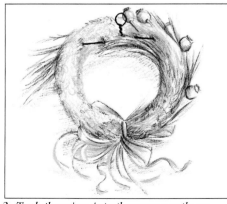

3 *Tuck the wires into the moss neatly on each side to secure.*

Making a plaited loop

Plait raffia strands in the same way as for a plaited raffia rope (see p.30). Loop the plaited raffia and bind the cross-over tightly with more raffia. Attach to a looped florist wire and insert the florist wire into the back of the base (see left).

Making a raffia loop

1 *Take two or three strands of raffia and fold the top of a florist wire over them. Twist the two ends of the wire together to make an "eye". Thread the florist wire needle through the base.*

2 *Pull the needle and raffia through the base, leaving a short end. Push the needle back through the base in the opposite direction. Cut the raffia from the needle and tie the two ends together to make a bow on top of the loop.*

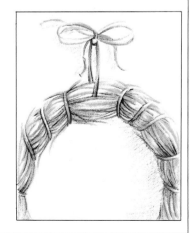

Tools, Materials and Containers

Dried-flower arranging requires the use of only a few simple pieces of equipment. With these well chosen tools you will be able to create an arrangement that both looks professional and is thoroughly enjoyable to make.

Cutting implements

The first essential piece of equipment is a good pair of florists' scissors. The scissors must be strong and sharp, for the stems of many plants, once they are throroughly dry, are tough to cut. It is useful to purchase scissors that can cut wire as well as flower stems. Otherwise, buy wire cutters for snipping florist wires and thinner wires. For much heavier stems a pair of pruning shears will come in handy. Do not use these for cutting wires, or you will blunt them very quickly. You will also need a long-bladed knife for cutting styrafoam blocks.

Wires for lengthening stems

Sometimes your dried flowers will be just the right length for your arrangement, or perhaps they will be longer than necessary and you will need to cut them down. However, they will often be too short and you will need to extend the length of the stems. To do this you will need florist wires or, for heavier plant material, sticks.

Florist wires are straight pieces of wire, available in a range of thicknesses and lengths. It is always best to use a wire that is just strong enough to support the flower-head that you attach it to, as this will look more natural. If you use too thick a wire, the artificial stem will be too rigid, and if you use too thin a wire, it will not be able to support the flower-head, foliage or seed-head without bending over.

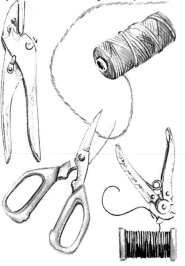

You can use this wire for single flower-heads or bunches. Attach the wire either with some thin spool wire or fine rose wire or by twisting the wire itself around the stem or stems. To disguise the false stem, cover florist wire and any attaching wire with binding tape, available in several stem colors and known as floral tape. This will make the wire stem look like the natural stem of the plant.

Material for supporting dried flowers

Frequently, dried flowers, seed-heads and foliage will not stand up in a container of their own accord and the stems must be supported. One way of achieving this is to put styrafoam into the container. You can simply wedge it in place, or, if the surface is very rough or porous, you can either glue it in position or secure it on prongs stuck to the bottom with adhesive clay (see p.19). Buy the styrafoam made specially for arranging dried flowers. It has a tougher texture than that used for supporting fresh flowers. Both the foam and adhesive clay, which comes in a roll, can be bought at most flower shops, garden centers or craft shops. Adhesive clay will stick to most surfaces, including shiny, glazed pottery and rough, textured baskets.

Instead of styrafoam you can place a pin holder at the base of a container to support the stems. However, the pins often do not seem to be in quite the right place to hold a stalk. This is always the case, it seems to me, when it is most important to have a flower in that very position.

Chicken wire is useful for supporting stems in a container with inward-curving sides. You will need to position at least a couple of separated layers of crumpled chicken wire to hold the stalks: one layer near the rim of the container.

Lentils or small dried beans also make good supporting material. Simply fill the container with the beans and push the stalks into them. They should be held quite firmly.

If you are using a lightweight container, then it is sensible to place some pebbles or adhesive clay at the bottom to weight the base, so that when the arrangement is completed it is not top heavy. Place at the sides of the styrafoam or pin holder, or underneath the chicken wire.

To make sure that the supporting substance is not visible once the arrangement is in place, cover the styrafoam or chicken wire with a layer of dried sphagnum moss or flower petals. Pot-pourri is ideal for this purpose and provides a sweet perfume, too.

Suitable containers

An enormous number of different types of container are suitable for arranging dried flowers and it is quite likely that you already have a good selection sitting at home, waiting to be used. There is no need to worry about whether a container is watertight. A wooden garden sieve, a cracked jug, a wicker basket, or a porous terracotta pot, all make perfectly good containers for a dried-flower arrangement. It is a good idea to keep a collection of containers ready to use for arrangements. Then, whenever you come across a container that appeals to you, simply add it to your collection. In this way, when you come to create a dried-flower arrangement you will usually be able to find just the right container to suit the type of arrangement and the position you want it to occupy.

Ceramic containers

You will probably not have to look too hard to find ceramic containers suitable for arrangements of flowers. Milk and cream jugs, casseroles and soufflé dishes, a cachepot, tea pot or coffee pot, a china soup or cereal bowl, a salad bowl or a sweetmeat dish, perhaps a biscuit barrel or a container for sugar or flour: all these can double as containers for dried flowers.

Keep an eye open for ceramic vases that appeal to you in antique or junk shops. It is still possible to find ceramic containers for a relatively small outlay that will look wonderful with dried flowers. In addition, flower shops, stores, gift and china shops all have good selections of ceramic vases to choose from in earthenware, stoneware, china and porcelain.

Bear in mind that because dried flowers tend to look informal and rustic, the most suitable containers are those which have the same qualities. So, ceramics with a very high gloss glaze are less suitable than those with a matt or eggshell finish. Sharply defined patterns lend themselves less well than softer or more primitive designs. Stoneware is a beautiful type of ceramic in which to arrange dried-plant material; its natural, stone-like quality complements almost any combination of dried flowers, foliage and seed-heads.

The warm colors of terracotta, the red, earthenware clay that is fired only once, seem to cry out for the rich hues of dried flowers, and the fact that the clay is porous does not, of course, matter at all. A simple flower-pot or saucer, or a strawberry pot or shallow seedling dish, can look just as effective when filled with glowing dried flowers as the more decorative and expensive pieces, such as

swagged pots and bowls. As terracotta ages, it takes on some beautiful colors, often developing a patina of silvery gray-green. This process can be greatly accelerated by standing the pot outside, exposing it to the elements. Terracotta can, however, develop faults if it is left outside in very severe cold. Such faults frequently do not become obvious until the weather becomes warmer, when the pots can simply fall to pieces.

Glass containers

Clear glass containers present a problem to the dried-flower arranger as the stems of dried flowers often do not look very attractive. However, there is a simple way to disguise the stems. Before arranging the flowers, fill the container with styrafoam, leaving about a 1cm ($\frac{1}{2}$in) gap between the glass and the foam. Then fill this space with an attractive dried material, such as moss, pot-pourri, flower petals or leaves (see p.19). There are no problems, of course, if the glass is opaque, or indeed if the flower stems are good-looking enough.

You may already have plenty of glass containers – glass jugs, tumblers, a decanter or a goldfish bowl. Otherwise, there is a wide selection of interesting glass vases to choose from in flower and gift shops. Plain cylindrical and rectangular clear glass vases make excellent containers for dried flowers, especially if their lining material can be related to the flowers in the arrangement.

Metal containers

The kitchen will provide inspiration here with cake and bread tins and maybe an ice bucket or metal salad bowl. If you are lucky, you will have a copper saucepan or casserole. The color of these containers makes them perfect for dried flowers. Decorated metal caddies or silver goblets are also possible dried-flower containers. Decorative boxes are often made out of metal either with painted designs or metal inlay. Brass and copper jardinières and cachepots can be bought from flower shops or garden centers.

Baskets

These are one of the best types of container for dried flowers. As they are made from dried material, they have a natural affinity with dried flowers, which means that it is difficult to go wrong if you choose one for an arrangement, to sit in any, save the most formal, position.

Hosts of baskets made in a wide range of

plant material are now available from flower shops and general stores. There are the familiar stems of willow, called osiers or withies, or twigs of hazel, birch, alder or ash; rushes and reeds are also traditional materials for baskets. Then there are more exotic materials, such as bamboo, palm, olive and gnarled vines, as well as some plant stems that perhaps you would not think of at first for making a basket. Lavender, thyme and broom twigs can all be woven into baskets and the first two have a wonderful scent, which will last for many months. They look good, too. Old baskets have a beautiful, well used quality, and you may find that you have an old shopping basket, waste-paper basket or log basket that can be brought into use again for a different purpose.

Wooden containers

It is more difficult to find wooden containers but, like wicker, they seem to be highly appropriate for dried-flower arrangements. A wooden garden sieve would be ideal, so would an old carved oak or elm box, an olive-wood salad bowl, or even a plain wooden plant tray or a box in which fruit or vegetables are packed. You may find that you have a painted or lacquered wooden button box or linen chest that you could use. However small the decoration on such a box, the colors might well suggest a scheme for an arrangement.

Adapting containers

Containers that are not very attractive in themselves, or that are cracked or dented, can be adapted both to conceal their faults and to suit a particular arrangement of dried flowers. Try weaving some of the dried material that is to be used in the arrangement into the framework of a basket to unify the arrangement and container. Twigs, moss, leafy stems and groups of flowers such as lavender and marjoram are all easy to incorporate in this way.

Most containers can be covered with a layer of moss or hay, or a combination of the two, together with some flowers. An ordinary, steep-sided plastic bucket can be treated in this way. Simply bind the moss or hay to the outside of the bucket with several lengths of raffia. If this is impossible because of the nature of the curve or slope of the container, then glue the moss or hay into place with a quick-drying adhesive. You can also cover containers with fabric, tatami, or fine woven matting.

Plant Guide

On the following pages you will find a wide selection of plants that can be effectively dried or preserved. Listed alphabetically by Latin name, each entry provides information on growing, drying and using dried-plant material, and indicates where the plant is featured.

Acacia dealbata
Mimosa, wattle
COLORS Yellow
PLANTING CONDITIONS Any soil, but not hardy in the North
TIME TO PICK Spring
METHODS OF DRYING Air dry hanging
HEIGHT Up to 1m (3ft)
PARTS TO USE Flowering branch
The flowering branches of mimosa air dry well, retaining both flower and leaf color extremely well. Use in arrangements to give a delicate, feathery effect and to offset stronger shapes.
FEATURED pp.17, 62

Acer spp.
Maple
COLORS Green, red, gold
PLANTING CONDITIONS Any soil, light position
PLANTING PLAN p.113
TIME TO PICK Summer or autumn
METHODS OF DRYING Press
HEIGHT 30cm (1ft)+
PARTS TO USE Leaf spray
Both the summer green and rich autumn foliage of maple can be dried by pressing under a carpet or rug.
FEATURED p.99

Achillea filipendulina
'Coronation Gold' and other varieties
Yarrow, milfoil
COLORS Yellow
PLANTING CONDITIONS Any soil, light position
PLANTING PLAN p.113
TIME TO PICK Summer
METHODS OF DRYING Air dry hanging or standing

HEIGHT 1m (3ft)
PARTS TO USE Flower-head
This hardy perennial produces saucer-shaped heads of bright yellow flowers which make a strong feature whether they are mixed with other dried flowers or used on their own in an arrangement.
FEATURED pp.29, 62, 63

Achillea millefolium 'Cerise Queen'
Yarrow
COLORS Pink
PLANTING CONDITIONS Any soil, light position
TIME TO PICK Summer
METHODS OF DRYING Air dry hanging
HEIGHT 60cm (2ft)
PARTS TO USE Flower-head
Although this yarrow dries to a dull pink, its flat heads of flowers are useful especially in mixed, rather subdued, cottagey arrangements.
FEATURED pp.12, 34

Alchemilla mollis
Lady's mantle
COLORS Gold
PLANTING CONDITIONS Any soil, light position
PLANTING PLAN pp.113, 125
TIME TO PICK Early summer
METHODS OF DRYING Air dry hanging
HEIGHT 30cm (1ft)
PARTS TO USE Flowering stem
Lady's mantle makes a very good filler with its filigree of tiny gold flowers. Its bright color enlivens the colors of the other dried flowers in the arrangement.
FEATURED pp.29, 91, 126

Allium afflatuense
Decorative or flowering onion
COLORS Pink
PLANTING CONDITIONS Any soil, light position
TIME TO PICK Summer
METHODS OF DRYING Air dry hanging or standing
HEIGHT 75cm (2ft 6in)
PARTS TO USE Flower-head, seed-head
Decorative onions dry easily and can be used for their flower- or seed-heads. For colorful balls of flowers, dry just as the buds start to open. For interesting texture allow the seed-heads to develop before picking.
FEATURED p.127

Alstromeria ligtu hybrid
Peruvian lily
COLORS Yellow, orange, red, pink
PLANTING CONDITIONS Any well-drained soil, sunny position
TIME TO PICK Summer
METHODS OF DRYING Dry with desiccant
HEIGHT 3cm ($\frac{3}{4}$in) flower
PARTS TO USE Flower
These delicate lilies dry with ease using desiccants.
FEATURED p.101

Amaranthus caudatus
'Viridis'
Love-lies-bleeding, prince's feather
COLORS Green
PLANTING CONDITIONS Any soil, light position
PLANTING PLAN p.125
TIME TO PICK Summer
METHODS OF DRYING Air dry hanging or standing
HEIGHT 30cm (1ft)
PARTS TO USE Flower spike
If dried hanging up, the tassel of the flowers dries straight. For a trailing effect, dry them upright. The bold, thin pyramid of flowers works well placed among softer and more

rounded material.
FEATURED p.127

Amaryllis belladonna
Belladonna lily
COLORS Pink red, white
PLANTING CONDITIONS Against sunny wall in well-drained soil, or grow in a pot
TIME TO PICK Autumn
METHODS OF DRYING Dry with desiccant
HEIGHT 12.5cm (5in) flower
PARTS TO USE Flower-head
These showy bulbs produce large, lily-like flowers in pink, red and white, that dry well using desiccants. Use in large, summery arrangements or float single heads on dry petals in a bowl.
FEATURED p.101

Ammobium alatum
Winged everlasting, sandflower
COLORS White
PLANTING CONDITIONS Any soil, light position
PLANTING PLAN p.125
TIME TO PICK Summer
METHODS OF DRYING Air dry hanging
HEIGHT 30cm (1ft)
PARTS TO USE Flower
These simple little daisy flowers retain a good white when dried. Unfortunately, they have thin stems near the flower-heads and tend to droop. Wire bunches if you wish them to stand upright in an arrangement, otherwise allow them to cascade on their own stems.
FEATURED pp.13, 97, 127

Anaphalis margaritacea
Pearly everlasting
COLORS White
PLANTING CONDITIONS Any soil, light position
PLANTING PLAN p.131
TIME TO PICK Summer
METHODS OF DRYING Air dry hanging or standing

HEIGHT 30cm (1ft)
PARTS TO USE Flower-head
The starry flowers of *Anaphalis margaritacea* are very simple with an informal shape. They look well in mixed posies and container arrangements.

Anemone coronaria
Anemone, windflower
COLORS Red, violet, white, yellow
PLANTING CONDITIONS Well-drained soil, light position
TIME TO PICK Spring, summer
METHODS OF DRYING Press or dry with desiccant
HEIGHT 3.5cm (1½in) flower
PARTS TO USE Flower
Anemones look particularly good when pressed for use in pressed-flower pictures. Otherwise, if dried with a desiccant, use them in arrangements like fresh anemones, or lay the flower-heads on top of a bowl of pot-pourri.
FEATURED p.99

Anethum graveolens
Dill
COLORS White
PLANTING CONDITIONS Any soil, light position
TIME TO PICK Summer
METHODS OF DRYING Air dry hanging
HEIGHT 45cm (18in)
PARTS TO USE Flower umbel
Dill flower-heads form a delicate tracery in arrangements. The stems retain their distinctive aromatic scent for a considerable time.
FEATURED pp.13, 29

Anigozanthos spp.
Kangaroo paw
COLORS Cream
PLANTING CONDITIONS Any soil, but not hardy in the North
TIME TO PICK Autumn
METHODS OF DRYING Air dry hanging
HEIGHT 45cm (18in)
PARTS TO USE Flower spike

The delicate little trumpet flowers of this tender Australian plant open from a rust-colored calyx, lending it a particular charm. Best suited to smaller arrangements, where it will look very fresh.
FEATURED p.79

Anthemis nobilis
Chamomile
COLORS White
PLANTING CONDITIONS Any soil, light position
TIME TO PICK Summer
METHODS OF DRYING Air dry hanging
HEIGHT 30cm (1ft)
PARTS TO USE Flower-head
The small center of the flower dries to a sturdy bobble. Make a stunning feature of the attractive dense hemispheres by dyeing them a bright color.
FEATURED p.107

Arundinaria spp.
Bamboo
COLORS Green
PLANTING CONDITIONS Any soil, but not all spp. hardy in North
PLANTING PLAN p.113
TIME TO PICK Summer
METHODS OF DRYING Air dry standing or lying flat
HEIGHT 1.8m (6ft) +
PARTS TO USE Leafy cane
Bamboo dries easily and its leaves turn a bluey-green as it dries. Ideal for large and medium-sized arrangements. *Arundinaria nitida* has small leaves.
FEATURED pp. 66, 67

Astilbe arendsii
Astilbe, goat's beard
COLORS Pink, cream, rust
PLANTING CONDITIONS Moist soil, light position
TIME TO PICK Summer
METHODS OF DRYING Air dry hanging
HEIGHT 60cm (2ft)
PARTS TO USE Flower panicle

The fine panicles of flowers in slender spires are most attractive in any kind of arrangement, and the soft cream, pink and rust flowers of astilbe blend well with most other dried flowers.

Athyrium filix-femina
Lady fern, female fern
COLORS Green
PLANTING CONDITIONS Any soil, shady position
PLANTING PLAN p.130
TIME TO PICK Summer
METHODS OF DRYING Press
HEIGHT 60cm (2ft)
PARTS TO USE Frond
The graceful fronds of lady fern look beautiful when used as a background to flowers or when featured with other foliage.
FEATURED pp.54, 55, 99

Avena fatua
Oats
COLORS Green
PLANTING CONDITIONS Any soil, sunny position
TIME TO PICK Summer
METHODS OF DRYING Air dry hanging or standing
HEIGHT 45cm (18in)
PARTS TO USE Seed-head
The delicate nodding heads of oats can be dried in their unripened green state or their ripened state, when they will be honey-colored.
FEATURED pp.54, 55, 97

Betula pendula
Birch
COLORS Brown
PLANTING CONDITIONS Any soil, light position
TIME TO PICK Winter
METHODS OF DRYING Air dry in position
HEIGHT 30cm–1.2m (1–4ft)
PARTS TO USE Twig
Twigs with catkins can be used to give a tracery of form to an arrangement, where they will dry naturally. Alternatively,

color twigs for Christmas decorations or use to make a wreath base.
FEATURED pp.26, 107

Briza media
Quaking grass
COLORS Green
PLANTING CONDITIONS Any soil, sunny position
TIME TO PICK Summer
METHODS OF DRYING Air dry standing or hanging
HEIGHT 30cm (1ft)
PARTS TO USE Seed-head
These small, nodding seed-heads give an interesting texture to an arrangement. Quaking grass makes a good filler.
FEATURED p.46

Bupleurum sp.
Bupleurum
COLORS White
PLANTING CONDITIONS Any soil, but not hardy in the North
TIME TO PICK Autumn
METHODS OF DRYING Air dry hanging
HEIGHT 30–60cm (1–2ft)
PARTS TO USE Flower-head, leaf
This tender Australian plant makes a good background filler, both for its green foliage and small white flower-heads.

Calendula officinalis
Pot marigold
COLORS Orange
PLANTING CONDITIONS Any soil, sunny position
PLANTING PLAN p.113
TIME TO PICK Summer
METHODS OF DRYING Air dry hanging
HEIGHT 22cm (9in)
PARTS TO USE Flower-head
Dry pot marigolds quickly in a warm airing cupboard or warming oven. Even so, the flowers have a tendency to disintegrate if they are not handled with extreme care. They have a strong color and look attractive in informal arrangements.

Callistemon subulatus
Bottlebrush
COLORS Red
PLANTING CONDITIONS Any soil,
but in mild climates only
TIME TO PICK Summer
METHODS OF DRYING Air dry
hanging
HEIGHT 30–60cm (1–2ft)
PARTS TO USE Flower, leaf
Bottlebrush provides one of
the best reds of any dried
flower. The little green leaves
offset the scarlet flower sta-
mens to give an exotic quality
to an arrangement.
FEATURED pp. 97, 114

Camellia japonica
Camellia
COLORS Red, pink, white,
green
PLANTING CONDITIONS Acid soil,
semi-shade. Not for far North
PLANTING PLAN p.130
TIME TO PICK Spring
METHODS OF DRYING Dry with
desiccant, crystallize, or
preserve with glycerine
HEIGHT Up to 7.5cm (3in)
flower; 45cm (18in) leaf spray
PARTS TO USE Flower, leaf
The flowers retain good color
and can be used as a major
ingredient in arrangements or,
if crystallized, as a decoration.
Leaf stems can be preserved in
glycerine, although they will
become very dark.
FEATURED p.105

Carlina acaulis
Carline thistle
COLORS White
PLANTING CONDITIONS Any soil,
sunny position
TIME TO PICK Autumn
METHODS OF DRYING Air dry
standing
HEIGHT 30cm (1ft)
PARTS TO USE Flower-head
These beautiful, but vicious,
large flower thistles, 10–15cm
(4–5in) across, are one of
the strongest-looking dried
flowers and, although they

have a wild look about them,
they suit both formal and informal arrangements.
FEATURED pp.13, 29, 97

Carthamus tinctorius
Safflower
COLORS Orange
PLANTING CONDITIONS Any soil,
sun, in mild climates
TIME TO PICK Summer
METHODS OF DRYING Air dry
hanging
HEIGHT 45cm (18in) spray
PARTS TO USE Flower, leaf stem
Pick just as the orange petals
begin to show for best dried
results. The flower color is
strong and safflower will show
well if arranged in groups. It is
worth drying safflower with
the upper leaves on the stem,
as they provide a good foil for
the flowers.
FEATURED pp.91, 97

Ceanothus 'A. T. Johnson'
Ceanothus
COLORS Blue
PLANTING CONDITIONS Well-
drained soil, sunny position,
but not hardy in North
PLANTING PLAN p.119
TIME TO PICK Early summer,
autumn
METHODS OF DRYING Dry with
desiccant
HEIGHT 13cm (5in) flower
spray
PARTS TO USE Flower
This ceanothus flowers twice,
once in early summer and
again in the autumn. Its flowers
are a marvellous blue color
and can make a striking addition to any arrangement.

Celosia cristata
Cockscomb
COLORS Red
PLANTING CONDITIONS Any soil,
sunny position
PLANTING PLAN p.125
TIME TO PICK Summer
METHODS OF DRYING Air dry
hanging

HEIGHT 30cm (1ft)
PARTS TO USE Flower-head
These extraordinary crested
flowers are, as their common
name implies, just like a cockscomb. Either use the whole
head for bold effect or wire
segments of the flower for a
more delicate effect.
FEATURED pp.12, 25, 126, 128

Centaurea cyanus
Cornflower
COLORS Blue
PLANTING CONDITIONS Any soil,
sunny position
PLANTING PLAN pp.119, 133
TIME TO PICK Summer
METHODS OF DRYING Air dry
hanging
HEIGHT 22cm (9in)
PARTS TO USE Flower
These intense blue corn-
flowers need to be dried in a
warm airing cupboard or
warming oven for best results.
One of the strongest blue
flowers available, they can
either be used in bunches in an
arrangement or they can be
mixed singly in more delicate
garden bouquets.
FEATURED pp.66, 68, 127

Centaurea macrocephala
Large-headed centaurea
COLORS Yellow
PLANTING CONDITIONS Any soil,
sunny position
TIME TO PICK Summer
METHODS OF DRYING Air dry
hanging
HEIGHT 45cm (18in)
PARTS TO USE Flower
Pick just as the yellow flowers
begin to open and retain some
of the upper foliage. These
strong-shaped flowers with
their globular bases and bright
yellow flowers are excellent for
large arrangements.
FEATURED pp.62, 63

Chaerophyllum temulentum
Chervil
COLORS White

PLANTING CONDITIONS Any soil,
light position
TIME TO PICK Summer
METHODS OF DRYING Press, or
air dry hanging or standing
HEIGHT 30cm (1ft)
PARTS TO USE Flower, seed-head
The flowering umbels of chervil and most similar umbellifer-
ous plants, such as fennel, cow
parsley and hogweed, can be
pressed to form beautiful
radiating patterns of stems and
flowers. The seed-heads can
also be air dried standing up or
hanging in bunches.
FEATURED p.99

Chenopodium ficifolium
Fig-leaved goose foot
COLORS Cream
PLANTING CONDITIONS Any soil,
light position
PLANTING PLAN p.133
TIME TO PICK Autumn
METHODS OF DRYING Air dry
standing
HEIGHT 1.2m (4ft)
PARTS TO USE Flowering stem
The large flowering stems of
this British native dry easily.
Use the flowering side spikes
as a filler, or use the whole
stems to make a dramatic im-
pact in large arrangements.

Choisya ternata
Mexican orange blossom
COLORS Green
PLANTING CONDITIONS Any soil,
but not hardy in North
TIME TO PICK Summer
METHODS OF DRYING Preserve in
glycerine
HEIGHT 30cm (1ft)
PARTS TO USE Leaf spray
The leaves are ideal for pre-
serving in glycerine as their
color does not deteriorate too
much. The leaf shape is inter-
esting and can look beautiful
with eucalyptus and beech.

Chrysanthemum
(*Tanacetum*) *vulgare*
Tansy

COLORS Yellow
PLANTING CONDITIONS Any soil, sunny position
TIME TO PICK Summer
METHODS OF DRYING Air dry hanging
HEIGHT 45cm (18in)
PARTS TO USE Flowering stem
Unlike its mum relatives, tansy air dries well. The little golden flowers are ideal for simple, natural-looking country arrangements.
FEATURED p.128

Cladonia sp.
Silver lichen
COLORS Silver
PLANTING CONDITIONS Acid soil, shady position
TIME TO PICK Any time
METHODS OF DRYING Air dry in a box or basket
HEIGHT 5cm (2in)
PARTS TO USE Whole plant hummock
Lichen is extremely versatile. It can be used as a base for dried-flower arrangements or as exterior cladding for wreaths, trees or any other shape. Alternatively, separate pieces can be wired and used in vase arrangements like flowers.
FEATURED pp. 50, 53, 76, 106, 107

Clematis vitalba
Old man's beard, traveller's joy
COLORS White
PLANTING CONDITIONS Any soil, light position
TIME TO PICK Late summer
METHODS OF DRYING Air dry hanging
HEIGHT 90cm (3ft) stem
PARTS TO USE Stem with seedhead
The beautiful whorled seedheads of many of the clematis genus make a striking addition to an arrangement. The stems twist interestingly and feature fascinating gnarled shapes.
FEATURED p.11

Cortaderia selloana
Pampas grass
COLORS Cream
PLANTING CONDITIONS Any soil, light position
TIME TO PICK Autumn
METHODS OF DRYING Air dry standing
HEIGHT 1.5m (5ft)
PARTS TO USE Flowering plume
Pick pampas plumes the moment they are fully formed and spray them with hair lacquer to prevent the seeds from dropping. Arrange by themselves, or with other grasses, or separate the sections of each plume and use in smaller arrangements.

Corylus avellana 'Contorta'
Corkscrew hazel
COLORS Brown
PLANTING CONDITIONS Any soil, light position
TIME TO PICK Winter
METHODS OF DRYING Air dry in position
HEIGHT 90cm (3ft)
PARTS TO USE Branch
The strange, contorted branches of this hazel will dry only if picked in winter. Color them for festive arrangements.
FEATURED p.87

Cotinus coggygria
Smoke bush, smoke tree
COLORS Brown
PLANTING CONDITIONS Any soil, light position
PLANTING PLAN p.131
TIME TO PICK Autumn
METHODS OF DRYING Air dry hanging
HEIGHT 45cm (18in)
PARTS TO USE Flowering inflorescence
The feathery panicles of the flowers leave their little stems in such a way as to give the impression that the shrub is covered with smoke. Remove the leaves on picking and use the flowers and stems to create a feathery, twiggy background.

Crocus chrysanthus
Crocus
COLORS Yellow, blue
PLANTING CONDITIONS Any soil, light position
TIME TO PICK Early spring
METHODS OF DRYING Dry with desiccant
HEIGHT 10cm (4in) flower
PARTS TO USE Flower
Wire each flower before drying with desiccants. A bowl of crocuses can look beautiful on their own.

Cucurbita maxima
Pumpkin
COLORS Orange
PLANTING CONDITIONS Rich soil, sunny position
TIME TO PICK Autumn
HEIGHT 30cm (1ft) +
PARTS TO USE Fruit
Hollow out pumpkins and carve faces into them to use at Hallowe'en. Insides are edible.
FEATURED p.81

Cucurbita pepo
Gourd
COLORS Orange, green, yellow
PLANTING CONDITIONS Any soil, sunny position
TIME TO PICK Autumn
METHODS OF DRYING Air dry standing
HEIGHT Up to 30cm (1ft)
PARTS TO USE Fruit
Cut when ripe and allow to dry out naturally in a dry atmosphere. Spray with lacquer to help preserve the fruit and retain the bright colors of the skin.
FEATURED pp.80, 81

Cynara scolymus
Globe artichoke
COLORS Green
PLANTING CONDITIONS Any soil, sunny position
TIME TO PICK Autumn
METHODS OF DRYING Air dry hanging or standing
HEIGHT 60cm (2ft) +
PARTS TO USE Flower-head

Pick globe artichokes either before the flower opens and dry the greeny brown head, or just as the flower begins to open and dry with its blue petals revealed. These large, striking, beautifully shaped heads lend themselves well to use in larger arrangements and can look wonderful when displayed singly.
FEATURED pp.45, 96

Cytisus scoparius
Scotch broom
COLORS Yellow, white, pink, green
PLANTING CONDITIONS Any soil, light position
METHODS OF DRYING Air dry hanging
HEIGHT 60cm (2ft) spray
PARTS TO USE Flower spray, stem
The delicate green stems of Scotch broom can be dried complete with pea-like flowers or without. Either way they make a fine, spiky effect in an arrangement.
FEATURED p.33

Dahlia sp.
Decorative dahlia and pompon dahlia
COLORS Red, yellow, white, pink, lilac
PLANTING CONDITIONS Any soil, sunny position
PLANTING PLAN p.113
TIME TO PICK Autumn
METHODS OF DRYING Air dry hanging, dry with desiccant
HEIGHT 30cm (1ft)
PARTS TO USE Flower-head
Close-knit petalled dahlias air dry well if picked about four days before the flowers reach perfection. Otherwise, providing they are in perfect condition, dry them with desiccants. Their warm autumnal colors and quilled petals lend strength to a delicate-looking arrangement.
FEATURED pp.12, 13, 23, 114, 115

Delphinium (Consolida)
ambigua
Annual larkspur
COLORS Pink, blue, white
PLANTING CONDITIONS Any soil,
sunny position
TIME TO PICK Summer
METHODS OF DRYING Air dry
hanging
HEIGHT 60cm (2ft)
PARTS TO USE Flower stem
One of the best dried flowers
for color and form. Larkspur
dries very easily and can be
used in almost any arrangement. Arrange them by themselves or mix them with other
flowers. Their brightly colored
spires provide interest in an
arrangement.
FEATURED pp.41, 54, 58, 62, 64,
121

Delphinium elatum
Larkspur
COLORS Blue, lilac, pink, white
PLANTING CONDITIONS Well-
drained soil, sunny position
TIME TO PICK Summer
METHODS OF DRYING Air dry
standing or hanging
HEIGHT 90cm–1.2m (3–4ft)
PARTS TO USE Flowering stem
The many hybrids of *Del-
phinium elatum* provide a
wide range of amazing colors,
from intense blues through
grays, lilacs and pinks to white.
They dry best in a cool, dark,
dry place standing in 7.5cm
(3in) of water, which slowly
evaporates. They can also be
hung to dry, but the flowers
will drop more readily. The
blues, in particular, look wonderful when set against the
bright green leaves of beech or
maple.
FEATURED pp.37, 58

Dryandra spp.
Dryandra
COLORS Yellow, green
PLANTING CONDITIONS Any soil,
sunny position; tender
TIME TO PICK Summer

METHODS OF DRYING Air dry
hanging
HEIGHT 30–60cm (1–2ft)
PARTS TO USE Flower, leaf
The flowers and leaves of the
Australian dryandras dry very
easily and can be used either as
a green foliage filler or, especially in informal arrangements,
for their thistle-like flowers.

Dryopteris filix-mas
Male fern
COLORS Green
PLANTING CONDITIONS Any soil,
shady position
TIME TO PICK Summer
METHODS OF DRYING Press
HEIGHT 60cm (2ft)
PARTS TO USE Frond
Fern fronds press very easily
and, because they grow in a
two-dimensional way, they
look perfectly natural when
used pressed in arrangements.

Echinops ritro
Globe thistle
COLORS Blue
PLANTING CONDITIONS Any soil,
sunny position
TIME TO PICK Summer
METHODS OF DRYING Air dry
hanging
HEIGHT 60cm (2ft)
PARTS TO USE Flower-head
Be careful to pick globe thist-
les before the flower develops
or it will fall to pieces when it is
dry and the gray-blue color will
fade. The strong globe shape
makes these thistles very dis-
tinctive in arrangements.
FEATURED pp.35, 54, 55, 58, 120

Elaeagnus pungens
Elaeagnus
COLORS Green
PLANTING CONDITIONS Any soil,
shady or sunny position
TIME TO PICK Summer
METHODS OF DRYING Preserve in
glycerine
HEIGHT 30cm (1ft)
PARTS TO USE Leaf spray
Like most evergreens, the leaf

sprays can be preserved in glycerine, but do not expect good
color results. Add green dye to
the glycerine to "help" the
color.

Erica arborea
Tree heather, tree heath
COLORS White
PLANTING CONDITIONS Moist,
lime-free soil, light position
PLANTING PLAN p.131
TIME TO PICK Spring
METHODS OF DRYING Air dry
hanging
HEIGHT 30–60cm (1–2ft)
flower spray
PARTS TO USE Flower-head
Pick just before the flowers
start to come out and spray
with hair lacquer before hang-
ing up to dry. Handle the love-
ly, textural, pinky-white spires
with their tiny leaves with care.
Left alone, they will last well in
an arrangement.
FEATURED p.35

Erodium cicutarium
Stork's bill, heron's bill
COLORS Green, pink
PLANTING CONDITIONS Any soil,
light position
TIME TO PICK Summer
METHODS OF DRYING Press
HEIGHT 5cm (2in)
PARTS TO USE Leaf, flower
Both the leaves and flowers of
erodiums and geraniums press
well. Use them with other
pressed flowers to create inter-
esting dried-flower pictures.
FEATURED p.99

Eryngium spp.
Sea holly
COLORS Blue
PLANTING CONDITIONS Any soil,
sunny position
PLANTING PLAN p.119
TIME TO PICK Late summer
METHODS OF DRYING Air dry
hanging
HEIGHT 60cm (2ft)
PARTS TO USE Thistle head, leaf
All the eryngiums have beauti-

ful gray-blue thistle flowers
that dry well. They lend a misty
character to arrangements and
some of the larger varieties
give strong form.
FEATURED p.22

Eucalyptus spp.
**Australian gum tree, cider
gum**
COLORS Silver
PLANTING CONDITIONS Any soil,
but for mild climates only
PLANTING PLAN p.119
TIME TO PICK Summer
METHODS OF DRYING Air dry
hanging, or preserve in
glycerine
HEIGHT 30–90cm (1–3ft)
PARTS TO USE Leaf spray
The silvery, mother-of-pearl-
colored leaves of all the eucalyptus genus can be either
air dried or preserved in glycerine. They are one of the
best subjects for the latter,
keeping good color. Dye can
be added to give good autumn
colors to the foliage.
FEATURED pp.11, 34, 41, 62, 103

Fagus sylvatica and variety
'Cuprea'
Beech
COLORS Green, rust
PLANTING CONDITIONS Any soil,
light position
TIME TO PICK Summer
METHODS OF DRYING Press, or
preserve in glycerine
HEIGHT 30–60cm (1–2ft)
PARTS TO USE Leaf stem
When pressed, the leaves of
common and copper beech
retain excellent color. Pick mature sprays of leaves in summer, whilst they still have the
fresh look that disappears in
early autumn. Copper beech
can be effectively preserved
with glycerine. Beech leaves
are wonderful when used as a
background to most flowers
and seed-heads, especially the
bright green pressed leaves.
FEATURED pp.11, 37, 47, 103

Fatsia japonica
False castor oil plant
COLORS Green
PLANTING CONDITIONS Any soil, shade, but mild climates only
PLANTING PLAN p.130
TIME TO PICK Summer
METHODS OF DRYING Press or preserve in glycerine
HEIGHT 20cm (8in)
PARTS TO USE Single leaf
The leaves are better pressed as they lose their color when preserved in glycerine. The pressed leaves are rather two-dimensional for use in arrangements but they can be interestingly used in pictures.
FEATURED p.103

Foeniculum vulgare
Common fennel
COLORS Green
PLANTING CONDITIONS Any soil, light position
PLANTING PLAN p.133
TIME TO PICK Summer
METHODS OF DRYING Air dry hanging
HEIGHT 90cm (3ft)
PARTS TO USE Seeding stem
The delicate seed formation of fennel looks rather like dill when dry and can be used for its feathery texture.

Freesia × kewensis
Freesia
COLORS Red, yellow, pink, blue, white
PLANTING CONDITIONS Well-drained soil, light position; tender
TIME TO PICK Summer
METHODS OF DRYING Dry with desiccant
HEIGHT 7.5cm (3in) flower spray
PARTS TO USE Flower spray
Freesias can look lovely arranged in a vase with some delicate greenery, such as callistemon or fern.
FEATURED p.100

Genista see Cytisus

Gentiana sino-ornata
Gentian
COLORS Blue
PLANTING CONDITIONS Well-drained, lime-free soil, sheltered position
TIME TO PICK Autumn
METHODS OF DRYING Dry with desiccant
HEIGHT 5cm (2in) flower
PARTS TO USE Flower
The incredible blue to which the plant gives its name is preserved when the flowers are dried with desiccants. Gentians look beautiful arranged by themselves in a low bowl.

Gomphrena globosa
Globe amaranth
COLORS Pink, white
PLANTING CONDITIONS Any soil, sunny position
TIME TO PICK Summer
METHODS OF DRYING Air dry hanging
HEIGHT 30cm (1ft)
PARTS TO USE Flowering stem
These pretty, clover-like flowers dry easily and look good used informally.

Grevillea rosmarinifolius
Australian spider bush
COLORS Green
PLANTING CONDITIONS Acid soil, sun and mild climate
TIME TO PICK Summer
METHODS OF DRYING Air dry hanging
HEIGHT 45cm (18in)
PARTS TO USE Leaf stem
Tender Australian grevilleas do not often flower in colder climates, but their foliage forms delicate spires when dried and is useful on its own.
FEATURED pp.62, 63

Grimmia pulvinata
Bun moss
COLORS Green
PLANTING CONDITIONS Acid soil, shady position
TIME TO PICK Summer
METHODS OF DRYING Air dry in basket or box
HEIGHT 3.5cm (1½in)
PARTS TO USE Hummock
Brilliant green mounds of moss make an ideal base for dried-flower trees.
FEATURED p.25

Gypsophila paniculata
Baby's breath
COLORS White
PLANTING CONDITIONS Any soil, sunny position
PLANTING PLAN pp.125, 131
TIME TO PICK Summer
METHODS OF DRYING Air dry standing or hanging
HEIGHT 30–60cm (1–2ft)
PARTS TO USE Spray of flowers
Gypsophila will dry well if left standing upright in a small amount of water, which soon evaporates. Its beautiful, delicate foam of white flowers makes a wonderful filler, and it also looks good arranged on its own.
FEATURED pp.33, 47, 127

Hedera helix
Ivy
COLORS Green
PLANTING CONDITIONS Any soil, light position
PLANTING PLAN pp.113, 119, 130
METHODS OF DRYING Press, or preserve in glycerine
HEIGHT 22cm (9in)
PARTS TO USE Spray of leaves
Ivy responds well to glycerine treatment but benefits from the addition of a little green dye to the glycerine solution.
FEATURED p.103

Helichrysum angustifolium
Curry plant
COLORS Yellow
PLANTING CONDITIONS Any soil, sunny position
PLANTING PLAN pp.113, 125
TIME TO PICK Summer
METHODS OF DRYING Air dry hanging
HEIGHT 22cm (9in)
PARTS TO USE Flower-head

This aromatic sub-shrub with silvery leaves has a good lemon color when dried. It looks very cottagey and is excellent in mixed garden arrangements.
FEATURED pp.29, 58, 114, 127, 128

Helichrysum bracteatum
Everlasting, strawflower
COLORS Red, pink, cream, yellow, white
PLANTING CONDITIONS Any soil, sunny position
PLANTING PLAN pp.113, 125
TIME TO PICK Summer
METHODS OF DRYING Air dry hanging
HEIGHT 45cm (18in)
PARTS TO USE Flower
Be sure to pick in bud just before the flowers start to open: the flowers will begin opening when they are hung up to dry. The most popular dried flower, the color and form when dried are excellent. However, the stem is rather weak and it is sometimes a good idea to wire the flower-heads before drying.
FEATURED pp.13, 33, 58, 66, 79, 86, 115, 126

Helichrysum italicum
Everlasting, strawflower
COLORS Yellow
PLANTING CONDITIONS Any soil, sunny position
TIME TO PICK Summer
METHODS OF DRYING Air dry hanging
HEIGHT 30cm (1ft)
PARTS TO USE Flower
These feature the strongest yellow of all dried flowers and have a very fresh look about them. However, the stems are rather weak and they usually need to be wired or propped up with other flowers in the arrangement.
FEATURED pp.66, 79

Helipterum manglesii
Sunray, everlasting daisy

COLORS Pink, white, yellow
PLANTING CONDITIONS Any soil, sunny position
PLANTING PLAN pp.119, 125
TIME TO PICK Summer
METHODS OF DRYING Air dry hanging
HEIGHT 30cm (1ft)
PARTS TO USE Flower
These delicate daisies are really fresh-looking, especially when grouped in bunches in an arrangement. Extremely versatile flowers, they look good in large and small arrangements, by themselves or mixed with other dried flowers.
FEATURED pp.22, 38, 39, 58

Helleborus spp.
Christmas rose, Lenten rose
COLORS Pink, white, green
PLANTING CONDITIONS Any moist soil, shady position
PLANTING PLAN pp.130, 133
TIME TO PICK Winter, spring
METHODS OF DRYING Dry with desiccant, press, or preserve in glycerine
HEIGHT 15cm (6in)
PARTS TO USE Flower, leaf
The beautiful hellebore flowers, ranging from the pure white of *H. niger* to the spotted greens, pinks and lilacs of *H. orientalis*, dry well with desiccants, or they can be pressed. The leaves can either be pressed or preserved in glycerine.
FEATURED p.7

Heracleum mantegazzianum
Giant hogweed
COLORS Brown
PLANTING CONDITIONS Rich, moist soil, light position
PLANTING PLAN p.133
TIME TO PICK Autumn
METHODS OF DRYING Air dry standing
HEIGHT 1.8m (6ft)
PARTS TO USE Seeding stem
The huge stems of giant hogweed, to which some people

are allergic, dry on the plant. They are very sturdy so they are not usually damaged by bad weather. They make a dramatic impression if used by themselves in a floor-standing arrangement. Umbels of seeds can be sprayed silver or gold and sprinkled with glitter for a pretty Christmas decoration.

Hosta spp. and cvs.
Plantain lily
COLORS Green
PLANTING CONDITIONS Moist but well-drained soil, shady position
PLANTING PLAN p.130
TIME TO PICK Summer
METHODS OF DRYING Press, or preserve in glycerine
HEIGHT Up to 45cm (18in)
PARTS TO USE Leaf, seeding stem
The distinctive leaves of hostas are their main attraction, although they have pretty white or lilac heads of flowers, followed by spikes of seed-heads. The pressed leaves make strong shapes in arrangements and those treated with glycerine act as a good foil to other, less solid, glycerined material such as eucalyptus.
FEATURED p.7

Humulus lupulus
Hops
COLORS Light green
PLANTING CONDITIONS Any soil, sunny position
TIME TO PICK Early autumn
METHODS OF DRYING Air dry hanging
HEIGHT Up to 3m (10ft)
PARTS TO USE Seed-head
Pick well before the heads ripen. Otherwise, they will fall to pieces as they dry. Hops tend to lose their color quickly once dry.
FEATURED p.34

Hydrangea macrophylla
Mop-headed or lace-cap hydrangea

COLORS Pink, rust, lilac, blue, green, white
PLANTING CONDITIONS Moist, well-drained soil, semi-shady position
PLANTING PLAN pp.119, 130
TIME TO PICK Autumn
METHODS OF DRYING Air dry hanging or standing, preserve in glycerine, or press
HEIGHT 22cm (9in) +
PARTS TO USE Flower-head
Hydrangeas are not easy to dry. They need to be picked just as the small true flowers at the center of each floret begin to open. They often dry best if arranged in a bowl with a little water, which soon evaporates. Whole heads of flowers or separate florets can be used.
FEATURED pp. 11, 23, 58, 66, 67, 98, 99, 101, 103, 120, 121

Ilex spp. and cvs.
Holly
COLORS Green
PLANTING CONDITIONS Any soil, light position
TIME TO PICK Summer
METHODS OF DRYING Preserve in glycerine
HEIGHT 30–60cm (1–2ft) spray
PARTS TO USE Leaf
Strong, serrated holly leaves are interesting to use in an arrangement, but the color of the leaves becomes very dark and heavy-looking after preserving in glycerine.
FEATURED p.103

Iris foetidissima
Stinking iris
COLORS Red
PLANTING CONDITIONS Any soil, light position
PLANTING PLAN p.133
TIME TO PICK Autumn
METHODS OF DRYING Air dry standing
HEIGHT 45cm (18in)
PARTS TO USE Seed-head
The dramatic seed-heads of this iris split in the autumn to reveal many bright orange

seeds. You can arrange stinking iris when fresh and simply leave it to dry in place.

Ixodia achilleoides
Ixodia
COLORS White
PLANTING CONDITIONS Any soil, sunny position
TIME TO PICK Summer
METHODS OF DRYING Air dry hanging
HEIGHT 30cm (1ft)
PARTS TO USE Flowering stem
The creamy white heads of the little, waxy daisy flowers are extremely pretty and have a very fresh look when dried. They mix well with all sorts of country-looking flowers.
FEATURED p.47

Kochia sp.
Silver cypress, summer cypress
COLORS Silver
PLANTING CONDITIONS Any soil, sunny position
METHODS OF DRYING Air dry hanging
HEIGHT 30–45cm (1–1½ft)
PARTS TO USE Leafy stem
The little silver succulent leaves of this kochia dry easily. The spikes of foliage are a wonderful foil to flowers, especially pastel-colored ones.
FEATURED pp.11, 41, 62, 120

Lachenalia aloides
Cape cowslip
COLORS Orange
PLANTING CONDITIONS Any soil, light position; tender
TIME TO PICK Winter
METHODS OF DRYING Press
HEIGHT 15cm (6in)
PARTS TO USE Flowering stem
The decorative bells with their spotted stems are pretty when used in a pressed-flower picture.
FEATURED p.99

Lavandula angustifolia
Lavender

COLORS Blue, mauve
PLANTING CONDITIONS Any soil, sunny position
PLANTING PLAN p.119
TIME TO PICK Summer
METHODS OF DRYING Air dry hanging
HEIGHT 30cm (1ft)
PARTS TO USE Flowering stem
It is most important to pick lavender just as the buds begin to show signs of opening. If you dry them any later than this, the flowers will simply drop off. Drying them fast in a warm airing cupboard helps to fix the flowers. They retain their wonderful scent for many months and clumps of lavender mixed with other flowers or used on their own look equally beautiful.
FEATURED pp.43, 121, 122

Leptospermum sp.
Silver strawberry, tea tree, ti tree
COLORS Red
PLANTING CONDITIONS Any soil, sun, but mild climates only
TIME TO PICK Summer
METHODS OF DRYING Air dry standing
HEIGHT 30cm (1ft)
PARTS TO USE Leaf, flower stem
The woody stems of silver strawberry have silver, felty leaves and a cluster of bright red flowers like helichrysum buds, which are very striking. They combine very attractively with pale pink flowers such as helipterum and helichrysum.
FEATURED pp.12, 33

Leucodendron rubrum
Leucodendron, tolbos, top-brush, silver bush
COLORS Brown, green, cream
PLANTING CONDITIONS Any soil, sunny position; tender
TIME TO PICK Summer
METHODS OF DRYING Air dry hanging or standing
HEIGHT 30cm (1ft)
PARTS TO USE Leaf, cone stem

These woody seeding cones, often growing on stems with pale greeny-silver leaves, are like flowers and have a strong form that looks very well in autumnal-colored arrangements.
FEATURED p.26

Liatris spicata
Kansas gayfeather, button snakeroot, blazing star, gayfeather
COLORS Purple, white
PLANTING CONDITIONS Any soil, light position
TIME TO PICK Summer
METHODS OF DRYING Air dry hanging
HEIGHT 45cm (18in)
PARTS TO USE Flowering stem
The long spikes are densely packed with flowers. Purple is not an easy color to use in arrangements and the white varieties tend to dry a rather gray/white.

Lilium spp. and cvs.
Lily
COLORS White, pink, orange, yellow
PLANTING CONDITIONS Well-drained rich soil, sunny or semi-shady position
TIME TO PICK Summer, autumn
METHODS OF DRYING Dry with desiccant, or press
HEIGHT Up to 20cm (8in) flower
PARTS TO USE Flower
These beautiful flowers can be dried well with desiccants and used stylishly in arrangements. *L. auratum* and *L. speciosum* are particularly good subjects.
FEATURED pp.60, 101

Limonium dumosum and *L. latifolium*
Sea lavender
COLORS White
PLANTING CONDITIONS Any soil, sunny position
TIME TO PICK Summer
METHODS OF DRYING Air dry

hanging or standing
HEIGHT 30cm (1ft)
PARTS TO USE Flower panicle
One of the most widely used dried flowers, sea lavender is useful as a background filler in arrangements. *Limonium latifolium* 'Blue Cloud' has delicate lilac-blue flowers. Sea lavender can look effective if lightly color-sprayed in pink, apricot or lemon, all of which look natural in arrangements.
FEATURED p.107

Limonium sinuatum
Statice
COLORS Purple, blue, white, yellow, pink, orange
PLANTING CONDITIONS Any soil, sunny position
TIME TO PICK Summer
METHODS OF DRYING Air dry hanging
HEIGHT 45cm (18in)
PARTS TO USE Flowering stem
A very popular dried flower. The color range available is enormous and you can buy seed that produces specific colors of flower. The triangular shape of the flowering head gives it a distinctive look in arrangements.
FEATURED pp.23, 47, 53, 68, 114

Limonium suworowii
Lamb's tail
COLORS Pink
PLANTING CONDITIONS Any soil, sunny position
TIME TO PICK Summer
METHODS OF DRYING Air dry hanging
HEIGHT 45cm (18in)
PARTS TO USE Flowering spike
The long tails of pink flowers are a very striking shape and yet they are delicate-looking, too. Take care not to break the dried stems as they are fragile.
FEATURED p.12

Lunaria rediviva
Honesty
COLORS Silver

PLANTING CONDITIONS Any soil, light position
TIME TO PICK Autumn
METHODS OF DRYING Air dry standing
HEIGHT 60cm (2ft)
PARTS TO USE Seed-head
The seed-heads of honesty can be used in their initial growing state when they are pinky-green. In addition, the outer filaments can be peeled away to reveal a silver disc to which the seeds adhere. These discs resemble mother-of-pearl and look very beautiful arranged by themselves or mixed with other dried material.

Magnolia spp.
Magnolia
COLORS Pink, white, green
PLANTING CONDITIONS Well-drained soil, light position
TIME TO PICK Spring, summer
METHODS OF DRYING Dry with desiccant, or preserve in glycerine
HEIGHT Up to 20cm (8in) flower
PARTS TO USE Flower, leaf
The magnificent magnolia flowers can be dried with desiccants and the glossy leaves of the evergreen *M. grandiflora* can be preserved in glycerine, when they turn almost black if no dye is added.

Mahonia japonica
Mahonia
COLORS Green
PLANTING CONDITIONS Any soil, shady position
TIME TO PICK Summer
METHODS OF DRYING Preserve in glycerine
HEIGHT 45cm (18in)
PARTS TO USE Leaf spray
The decorative and geometric-shaped mahonia leaves are rather prickly, but when preserved in glycerine are easy to arrange. They act as a foil to more rounded, soft material.
FEATURED p.7

Malus sylvestris
Apple, crab apple
COLORS Brown
PLANTING CONDITIONS Any soil, sunny position
TIME TO PICK Winter
METHODS OF DRYING Air dry in position
HEIGHT 60cm (2ft)
PARTS TO USE Twig
Cut and dry the branches and twigs of deciduous trees during the winter. Apple trees have interestingly shaped branches.
FEATURED p.57

Matteucia struthiopteris
(*Struthiopteris germanica*)
Ostrich feather fern
COLORS Green
PLANTING CONDITIONS Moist but well-drained soil, shady position
PLANTING PLAN p.131
TIME TO PICK Summer
METHODS OF DRYING Press
HEIGHT 1m (3ft)
PARTS TO USE Whole frond
The fronds of this beautiful fern, which grows like a shuttlecock, can easily be dried under a carpet or rug, then used like fresh fern.

Miscanthus sinensis
Miscanthus
COLORS Brown
PLANTING CONDITIONS Any soil, sunny position
PLANTING PLAN p.133
TIME TO PICK Autumn
METHODS OF DRYING Air dry hanging or standing
HEIGHT 1.5m (5ft)
PARTS TO USE Leaf, seed frond
The blue-green leaves and fronds dry to a beige color but look beautiful springing from a large arrangement.

Moluccella laevis
Bells of Ireland, Irish green bells, shell flower
COLORS Cream
PLANTING CONDITIONS Rich soil, sunny position
PLANTING PLAN p.131
TIME TO PICK Summer
METHODS OF DRYING Preserve in glycerine
HEIGHT 60cm (2ft)
PARTS TO USE Flowering stem
The interesting part of the moluccella plant is the calyx from which the sweetly scented but insignificant flowers grow. The flowers should be picked just as the first ones begin to emerge and preserved in glycerine solution. They will turn a pale, creamy color.
FEATURED pp.11, 102

Narcissus spp. and cvs.
Daffodil
COLORS Yellow, white
PLANTING CONDITIONS Any soil, light position
PLANTING PLAN p.133
TIME TO PICK Spring
METHODS OF DRYING Dry with desiccant, crystallize
HEIGHT 1–7.5cm ($\frac{1}{2}$–3in) flower
PARTS TO USE Flower
The flowers of most bulbs can be dried with desiccants. Narcissus dry very well, but usually look best arranged either by themselves or with flowers of the same season.
FEATURED pp.101, 104, 105

Nigella damascena
Love-in-a-mist
COLORS Blue, green
PLANTING CONDITIONS Any soil, sunny position
PLANTING PLAN p. 125
TIME TO PICK Summer, early autumn
METHODS OF DRYING Air dry hanging
HEIGHT 45cm (18in)
PARTS TO USE Seed-head, flower
The almost spherical seed-heads of nigella are extremely beautiful and dry easily. The flowers, which are a very pale blue, can also be dried but, like cornflowers, they need to' be

placed in a warm airing cupboard or warming oven for best color results.
FEATURED pp.43, 47, 127

Origanum majorana
Marjoram
COLORS Rust
PLANTING CONDITIONS Any soil, sunny position
TIME TO PICK Summer
METHODS OF DRYING Air dry hanging
HEIGHT 22cm (9in)
PARTS TO USE Flowering stem
Not only is this herb pretty to look at but it will scent an arrangement deliciously.
FEATURED p.13

Osmunda regalis
Royal fern
COLORS Green
PLANTING CONDITIONS Moist soil, shady position
TIME TO PICK Summer
METHODS OF DRYING Press
HEIGHT 1.2m (4ft)
PARTS TO USE Frond
This magnificent fern with its huge, pale green fronds can be used either whole for very large arrangements or broken into small leaf sections for quite small ones. It is one of the most versatile ferns and lacks only in not being evergreen.
FEATURED pp.11, 59

Paeonia lactiflora
Peony
COLORS Pink, white, cream, red
PLANTING CONDITIONS Any well-drained soil, sunny position
TIME TO PICK Summer
METHODS OF DRYING Dry with desiccant, or air dry hanging
HEIGHT 45cm (18in) flowering stem
PARTS TO USE Flower
These are sumptuous flowers and, if dried with desiccants, they closely resemble their fresh counterparts. The double varieties can also be air

dried: hang them just as the bud begins to open. They look wonderful in any arrangement and they seem to epitomize the beginning of summer.
FEATURED pp.59, 101, 120, 121

Papaver rhoeas
Field poppy
COLORS Gray, green
PLANTING CONDITIONS Any soil, sunny position
PLANTING PLAN p.133
TIME TO PICK Summer
METHODS OF DRYING Air dry hanging or standing
HEIGHT 60cm (2ft)
PARTS TO USE Seed-head
The strong form of poppy seed-heads makes them a favorite for use in dried-flower arrangements. Color them red, green, silver or gold and use at Christmas.
FEATURED pp.41, 43

Phaenocoma prolifera
Phaenocoma shrub
COLORS Pink
PLANTING CONDITIONS Any soil, sunny position
TIME TO PICK Summer
METHODS OF DRYING Air dry hanging
HEIGHT 30cm (1ft)
PARTS TO USE Flowering stem
The flowers are a particularly vivid pink, stronger than both helipterum and helichrysum, both of which they resemble. They are set off by the tiny silver gray leaves.
FEATURED pp.47, 66

Phlomis fruticosa
Jerusalem sage
COLORS Yellow, gray
PLANTING CONDITIONS Any soil, sunny position, mild climates
TIME TO PICK Summer
METHODS OF DRYING Air dry hanging
HEIGHT 45cm (18in)
PARTS TO USE Leaf, flower, seed-head
Pick phlomis either as the yel-

low flowers start to open, and dry it for both the foliage and flowers, or wait until the whorls of seeds appear and dry the leaves and seed-heads. Either way, the dried plant is attractive and has a distinctly Mediterranean look.

Physalis alkekengi
Chinese lantern, bladder cherry, Cape gooseberry
COLORS Orange
PLANTING CONDITIONS Any soil, sunny position
TIME TO PICK Autumn
METHODS OF DRYING Air dry hanging
HEIGHT 60cm (2ft)
PARTS TO USE Seed-head
The little fruits of physalis are covered by a papery filament that resembles a bright orange lantern. The brilliant color brightens even the darkest corners of a room. The lantern can be cut open to make the filament resemble the petals of a flower.
FEATURED pp.65, 85

Picea pungens 'Glauca'
Silver spruce, blue spruce
COLORS Silver-blue
PLANTING CONDITIONS Acid soil, light position
TIME TO PICK Any time
METHODS OF DRYING Air dry in position
HEIGHT 15cm (6in)
PARTS TO USE Spray
Silver spruce is very useful for Christmas decorations, as it dries to look almost identical to the fresh foliage and can therefore be used well in advance. Of course, it can also be used in arrangements at other times of the year.
FEATURED pp.85, 86

Pinus sylvestris
Scots pine
COLORS Green
PLANTING CONDITIONS Acid soil, light position

TIME TO PICK Any time
METHODS OF DRYING Air dry standing
HEIGHT 60cm (2ft)
PARTS TO USE Spray of needles
Scots pine dries well, retaining its color and dropping only a very few needles.
FEATURED p.87

Pithocarpa corymbulosa
Miniature daisy
COLORS White
PLANTING CONDITIONS Any soil, sunny position
TIME TO PICK Summer
METHODS OF DRYING Air dry hanging
HEIGHT 45cm (18in)
PARTS TO USE Flowering stem
These little white daisies are almost as delicate as gypsophila, but each flower has a more marked daisy shape. Very pretty and ideal for fresh, frothy arrangements.
FEATURED p.79

Polygonatum multiflorum
Solomon's seal
COLORS White
PLANTING CONDITIONS Any soil, shady position
PLANTING PLAN p.133
TIME TO PICK Spring
METHODS OF DRYING Dry with desiccants, or preserve in glycerine
HEIGHT 45cm (18in)
PARTS TO USE Flowering stem
Both the nodding white flowers and pale green leaves can be dried with desiccants or preserved with glycerine. The gracious, arching stems make beautiful shapes in arrangements and look particularly good with other shade-loving plants such as ferns, hostas and Christmas roses.

Polystichum setiferum plumoso-divisilobum
Shield fern
COLORS Green
PLANTING CONDITIONS Moist soil,

shady position
TIME TO PICK Summer
METHODS OF DRYING Press
HEIGHT 45cm (18in)
PARTS TO USE Frond
This evergreen fern is very finely divided and looks almost feather-like. The fronds are very attractive and look good set amongst any other dried flowers.

Primula vulgaris
Primrose
COLORS Yellow, white, pink
PLANTING CONDITIONS Moist soil, light position
PLANTING PLAN p.133
TIME TO PICK Spring
METHODS OF DRYING Dry with desiccant, press, or crystallize
HEIGHT 5cm (2in)
PARTS TO USE Flower
The tiny, fragile primrose flowers can be equally well dried with desiccants, pressed or crystallized, when they are delicious to eat.
FEATURED pp.104, 105

Protea spp.
Protea
COLORS Pink, brown
PLANTING CONDITIONS Any soil, sunny position; tender
TIME TO PICK Summer
METHODS OF DRYING Air dry hanging
HEIGHT 30cm (1ft) +
PARTS TO USE Flower
Proteas need to be picked just as the bud begins to open and hung to dry: the flower will continue to open so that once dry it will look perfect.
FEATURED p.109

Prunus spp. and cvs.
Almond, peach, nectarine, cherry
COLORS Pink, white
PLANTING CONDITIONS Any soil, sunny position
PLANTING PLAN p.133
TIME TO PICK Spring
METHODS OF DRYING Crystallize

HEIGHT 12mm ($\frac{1}{2}$in) flower
PARTS TO USE Single flower
The flowers of almond, peach, nectarine and cherry are delicious when crystallized.
FEATURED pp.104, 105

Pulmonaria saccharata
Bethlehem sage
COLORS Pink, blue
PLANTING CONDITIONS Any soil, shady position
TIME TO PICK Spring
METHODS OF DRYING Crystallize
HEIGHT 2.5cm (1in) flower
PARTS TO USE Flowering stem
These pretty plants with spotted leaves flower in early spring. When crystallized, the flowering sprays make an attractive decoration for a cake.
FEATURED p.104

Quercus palustris
Pin oak
COLORS Green, rust
PLANTING CONDITIONS Any soil, light position
TIME TO PICK Summer, autumn
METHODS OF DRYING Press
HEIGHT 60cm (2ft) spray
PARTS TO USE Leaf spray
All oak leaves press well under a rug or carpet. Either press the leaves in summer when they are green or in the autumn, as they begin to change color.
FEATURED p.32

Ranunculus asiaticus
Persian buttercup
COLORS Yellow, red, pink, white, orange
PLANTING CONDITIONS Moist soil, sunny position
TIME TO PICK Early summer
METHODS OF DRYING Dry with desiccant, or air dry hanging
HEIGHT 30cm (1ft)
PARTS TO USE Flower
Related to the buttercup, which can also be dried, ranunculus look like miniature peonies. Their many colors

make them exciting to use in informal arrangements.
FEATURED p.101

Rosa spp. and cvs.
Rose
COLORS Red, pink, yellow, cream, orange, white, lilac
PLANTING CONDITIONS Well-drained soil, sunny position
PLANTING PLAN pp.113, 119, 125, 130, 131
TIME TO PICK Summer
METHODS OF DRYING Air dry hanging or dry with desiccant
HEIGHT 15–45cm (6–18in)
PARTS TO USE Flower
The most well known and best loved flower of all. Hybrid tea roses air dry well when hung in a cool, dry, dark place. Single roses and double, old-fashioned roses must be dried with desiccants for best results.
FEATURED pp.10, 12, 17, 29, 50, 51, 53, 58, 60, 66, 73, 97, 101, 105, 115, 121, 126

Rumex obtusifolius
Dock, sorrel
COLORS Rust
PLANTING CONDITIONS Any soil, light position
TIME TO PICK Summer
METHODS OF DRYING Air dry standing
HEIGHT 1.2m (4ft)
PARTS TO USE Seeding stem
Dock stems dry to a rich, rust-green color. Use the whole seeding stems in large arrangements or break each stem into small pieces and use in both small and medium-sized arrangements.
FEATURED p.97

Salvia spp. and cvs.
Sage
COLORS Purple, pink
PLANTING CONDITIONS Any soil, sunny position
TIME TO PICK Summer
METHODS OF DRYING Air dry hanging

HEIGHT 30cm (1ft)
PARTS TO USE Flower, bract, leaf
Many salvias, including cottagey 'Clary', dry well. *Salvia farinacea* looks rather like rich-colored lavender when dried.
FEATURED p.47

Santolina spp.
Lavender cotton
COLORS Silver, yellow
PLANTING CONDITIONS Any soil, sunny position
PLANTING PLAN p.131
TIME TO PICK Summer
METHODS OF DRYING Air dry hanging
HEIGHT 30cm (1ft)
PARTS TO USE Foliage, flower spray
Both the flowers and silvery foliage of santolinas dry well. *S. neapolitana* is particularly good for drying. Their aromatic foliage lends an attractive scent to dried arrangements.
FEATURED pp.62, 63

Scabiosa atropurpurea
Cottage scabious, sweet scabious
COLORS Blue, purple, white
PLANTING CONDITIONS Any soil, sunny position
PLANTING PLAN p.133
TIME TO PICK Summer, autumn
METHODS OF DRYING Air dry hanging
HEIGHT 30cm (1ft)
PARTS TO USE Flower
Although the flowers shrink substantially as they dry, they still look attractive in their subtle, dusty colors.
FEATURED p.13

Scilla sibirica
Squill
COLORS Blue
PLANTING CONDITIONS Any soil, sunny position
TIME TO PICK Spring
METHODS OF DRYING Dry with desiccant, or crystallize
HEIGHT 10cm (4in)

PARTS TO USE Flower spray
Little scillas are a wonderful blue color. They can be dried using desiccants or preserved in sugar and used as a decoration on a cake or tart.
FEATURED p.105

Sedum spectabile
Spectacular sedum
COLORS Pink
PLANTING CONDITIONS Well-drained soil, sunny position
PLANTING PLAN p.131
TIME TO PICK Autumn
METHODS OF DRYING Air dry hanging
HEIGHT 30cm (1ft)
PARTS TO USE Flower-head
The mounded pink florets of sedums will dry eventually, although it takes a long time for the moisture to go from the fleshy stems. If they become too brown they can be spray-painted lightly to their natural pink color.

Selaginella sp.
Club moss
COLORS Green
PLANTING CONDITIONS Moist soil, light position
TIME TO PICK Any time
METHODS OF DRYING Air dry, or preserve in glycerine
HEIGHT 5cm (2in)
PARTS TO USE Whole plant
This is a plant that looks good preserved in a glycerine solution to which green dye has been added. The green dye keeps it close to its natural, bright green color. Club moss can be used as a base for arrangements or bunches can be used like foliage.
FEATURED p.102

Senecio greyi
Senecio, German ivy
COLORS Silver
PLANTING CONDITIONS Any soil, light position
PLANTING PLAN p.119
TIME TO PICK Summer

METHODS OF DRYING Air dry hanging, or press
HEIGHT 30cm (1ft)
PARTS TO USE Leaf, flower bud
Senecio greyi should be picked well before the yellow flowers begin to open, as it is the leaves and buds which are attractive when dried.
FEATURED pp.16, 38, 39, 58, 98, 120

Silene pendula
Campion, pink cluster daisy, nodding catchfly
COLORS Pink
PLANTING CONDITIONS Any soil, sunny position
TIME TO PICK Summer
METHODS OF DRYING Air dry hanging
HEIGHT 30cm (1ft)
PARTS TO USE Flower
The delicate little pale pink flowers of this garden campion look very fresh when dried.
FEATURED pp.12, 50, 51, 79

Solidago canadensis
Golden rod
COLORS Yellow, green
PLANTING CONDITIONS Any soil, light position
PLANTING PLAN p.131

TIME TO PICK Autumn
METHODS OF DRYING Air dry hanging
HEIGHT 60cm–1m (2–3ft)
PARTS TO USE Flower spray
The many forms of golden rod, all of which dry well, vary considerably, some having close-knit "feathers" of flowers and others having more open plumes. You can also dry them well before the flowers open to use when green.
FEATURED pp.25, 97, 115, 117

Sphagnum sp.
Sphagnum moss
COLORS Green
PLANTING CONDITIONS Moist, acid soil, light position
TIME TO PICK Any time

METHODS OF DRYING Air dry
HEIGHT 7.5cm (3in)
PARTS TO USE Whole plant
Invaluable as a base for many
types of arrangement.
FEATURED p.58

Stachys lanata
Lamb's ear, lamb's tongue
COLORS Silver
PLANTING CONDITIONS Any soil,
sunny position
PLANTING PLAN p.119
METHODS OF DRYING Air dry
hanging, or press
HEIGHT 22cm (9in)
PARTS TO USE Flower bud spray,
leaf
The woolly silver bud sprays
have a very strong form.
FEATURED pp.98, 99, 121, 123

Taxus baccata
Yew
COLORS Green
PLANTING CONDITIONS Any soil,
light position
TIME TO PICK Any time
METHODS OF DRYING Air dry
hanging or standing
HEIGHT 15–60cm (6in–2ft)
spray
PARTS TO USE Foliage spray
Yew dries well without drop-
ping and it can be used both in
Christmas arrangements or as
foliage in all-year-round dis-
plays.

Tilia cordata
Lime, linden
COLORS Green, rust
PLANTING CONDITIONS Any soil,
light position
TIME TO PICK Summer
METHODS OF DRYING Air dry, or
preserve in glycerine
HEIGHT 30cm (1ft)
PARTS TO USE Seeding spray
The color of the seed sprays
can be enhanced with the ad-
dition of rust-colored dye to
the glycerine solution, which
will lend autumnal tints to the
material.
FEATURED p.102

Tillandsia usneoides
Tumbleweed, Spanish moss
COLORS Gray
PLANTING CONDITIONS Epiphytic;
tender; common in South
TIME TO PICK Any time
METHODS OF DRYING Air dry
hanging
HEIGHT 20cm (8in)
PARTS TO USE Strand
This extraordinary plant looks
like narrow gray hay. It makes a
lace-like surround for posies
and ropes and can also be
used to cover frames and
bases.
FEATURED pp.17, 33

Tulipa spp. and cvs.
Tulip
COLORS Red, yellow, pink,
white, purple
PLANTING CONDITIONS Any soil,
sunny position
TIME TO PICK Spring
METHODS OF DRYING Dry with
desiccant
HEIGHT 7.5–10cm (3–4in)
flower
PARTS TO USE Flower-head
All tulips – single, double and
parrot – can be dried effec-
tively with desiccants and used
to striking effect.
FEATURED p.101

Typha angustifolia
Bulrush, reedmace, cat-tail
COLORS Brown
PLANTING CONDITIONS Rich
loam, water
PLANTING PLAN p. 133
TIME TO PICK Autumn
METHODS OF DRYING Air dry
standing
HEIGHT 1–1.2m (3–4ft)
PARTS TO USE Seed-head
Bulrushes must be picked just
as the roll of seeds turns
brown, and well before the
column starts to break up and
deposit its seeds. Spray the
surface of the bulrush with
lacquer to hold the seeds in
position as it dries.
FEATURED p.11

Verticordia brownii
'Morrison'
**Feather flower, cauliflower
morrison**
COLORS Cream
PLANTING CONDITIONS Any soil,
sunny position
TIME TO PICK Summer
METHODS OF DRYING Air dry
hanging
HEIGHT 45cm (18in)
PARTS TO USE Flower corymb
The strong-shaped, large, flat
corymbs of flowers, which dry
easily, add an interesting tex-
ture to arrangements.
FEATURED p.41

Viola spp.
Violet, pansy
COLORS Violet
PLANTING CONDITIONS Moist soil,
light position to part shade
PLANTING PLAN p.133
TIME TO PICK Spring
METHODS OF DRYING Press, or
crystallize
HEIGHT 5cm (2in)
PARTS TO USE Flower
The scented violet is delicious
to eat when it has been crystal-
lized, either using the gum-
arabic or egg-white method.
FEATURED pp.98, 99

Vitis spp. and cvs.
Grape
COLORS Brown
PLANTING CONDITIONS Well-
drained soil, light position
TIME TO PICK Winter
METHODS OF DRYING Air dry
standing
HEIGHT 1.2m (4ft)
PARTS TO USE Grape stem
Grape stems can be twisted
together in lengths of about
1.2m (4ft) to form rustic-
looking wreaths. Bend into
shape before the woody stems
dry out so they do not snap
before they are in place.

Xeranthemum sp.
Common immortelle
COLORS Lilac, white

PLANTING CONDITIONS Any soil,
sunny position
TIME TO PICK Summer
METHODS OF DRYING Air dry
hanging
HEIGHT 45cm (18in)
PARTS TO USE Flowering stem
The papery flowers of immortelle will dry on the plant, but
they are very delicate and often
get damaged if dried in this
way.
FEATURED pp.12, 58

Zea mays
Corn-on-the-cob
COLORS Orange, yellow, purple
PLANTING CONDITIONS Rich soil,
sunny position
TIME TO PICK Summer, autumn
METHODS OF DRYING Air dry
standing
HEIGHT 30cm–1.5m (1–5ft)
PARTS TO USE Seed-head
There are many varieties of
corn-on-the-cob or Indian
corn. The 'Rainbow' variety
produces a selection of small
different colored cobs which
are not edible.
FEATURED pp.11, 97

Zinnia elegans
Zinnia
COLORS Yellow, orange, red,
cream
PLANTING CONDITIONS Well-
drained soil, sunny position
TIME TO PICK Summer
METHODS OF DRYING Dry with
desiccant
HEIGHT 5cm (2in) flower
PARTS TO USE Flower-head
These half-hardy annuals from
Mexico dry very well with de-
siccants. Their brilliant colors
are well suited to strong,
autumnal arrangements.

Index

Acknowledgments

Author's acknowledgments
I would like to thank photographer Andreas Einsiedel, art editor Sally Smallwood, and editor Jane Laing for all their inspirational help in producing this book. Very special thanks to Sue Newth for such wonderful support, together with all the staff at Hillier and Hilton, 98 Church Road, London SW13. Also thanks to Stephen Bennington, May Cristea, Kathleen Darby, Peter Day, June Henry, Veronica Hitchcock, Peter Machin, Jay Musson, Jenny and Richard Raworth, Alex Starkey, Josephine White, and Roddy Wood.

Dorling Kindersley would like to thank Richard Bird for the index, Lynn Bresler for proof-reading, Jenny Engelman and Kate Grant for their enormous help with typing, Osborne and Little for supplying fabric and wallpaper (pages 59–61), Christian Tumpling for photographic assistance, and Rupert Wheeler for his invaluable help with the production of the book.

Illustrators
Andrew MacDonald: pages 20, 113, 119, 125, 130/1, 133
Lesli Sternberg: pages 14/15, 19, 21, 24, 27/8, 30/1, 137–43